# THE NEW BOOK OF
# *Pasta*

# THE NEW BOOK OF
# *Pasta*

## ANNE SHEASBY

PHOTOGRAPHED BY
## PATRICK McLEAVEY

PUBLISHED BY
SALAMANDER BOOKS LIMITED
LONDON

Published by Salamander Books Limited
8 Blenheim Court, Brewery Road, London N7 9NY

9 8 7 6 5 4 3 2 1

© Salamander Books Ltd., 2002

A member of the Chrysalis Group plc

ISBN 1 84065 223 3

Project managed by: Stella Caldwell
Editor: Madeline Weston
Designer: Sue Storey
Photographer: Patrick McLeavey
Photographer's Assistant: Rebecca Willis
Home Economist: Sandra Miles
Production: Phillip Chamberlain
Filmset and reproduction by: Anorax Imaging, England

Printed in Spain

# CONTENTS

# INTRODUCTION

Pasta has formed an important part of the Italian diet for centuries, but it is also a very popular food across the world and is ideal for today's busy cooks. The wide range of fresh and dried pasta is impressive and the shapes and types of pasta readily available ensure that you have plenty of choice when it comes to selecting which pasta to cook.

Pasta also plays an important role in a healthy, well-balanced diet. It is a nutritious food – it is low in fat and provides a good source of carbohydrate and, hence, is a valuable source of energy. Pasta also provides a useful source of protein and some vitamins and minerals.

The word pasta literally means 'dough' or 'paste'. Pasta is made from a basic mixture of durum (hard) wheat flour and water to which other flavourings or colours may be added. A slightly richer type of pasta known as egg pasta or *pasta all'uova* is also commonly available and this is a simple mixture of wheat flour, eggs, water and sometimes olive oil. Egg pasta tends to be slightly darker in colour than the paler basic durum wheat pasta.

The basic pasta dough may then be flavoured or coloured in various ways and common flavourings include spinach (which colours pasta pale green and is known as *pasta verde*), garlic and chopped herbs or chopped basil, garlic and chilli, tomato purée (pale reddish-orange pasta known as *pasta rossa*), black olives, squid ink (black pasta), mushrooms or porcini (pale brown pasta), beetroot (deep pink pasta) or saffron (which colours pasta a deep yellow).

Wholewheat varieties of pasta are also available. These are darker brown in colour and have a slightly chewier texture. Wholewheat pasta also contains more dietary fibre than white pasta.

There are also many varieties of filled or stuffed pasta for us to enjoy, including ravioli, tortellini, tortelloni, etc. These include various fillings, ranging from the classic minced meat, spinach and ricotta or mixed cheese fillings to other flavour combinations such as smoked ham and cheese or mushroom and ricotta. Again, filled or stuffed pasta are readily available in fresh or dried forms.

Organic pasta is becoming more obtainable, and speciality pasta such as gluten-free or wheat-free pasta including rice pasta, buckwheat pasta, barley pasta and corn pasta, as well as egg-free and low-protein pasta are also available in health food stores.

An extensive range of both dried and fresh pasta is readily obtainable in many of our supermarkets, delicatessens and local shops. It is worth visiting a good Italian delicatessen if you can, as they often sell a selection of pasta which is freshly made on the premises.

## TYPES AND SHAPES OF PASTA

Pasta comes in a vast array of shapes and sizes, some of which are specific to one type of dish such as cannelloni tubes or large pasta shells (called *conchiglie rigate*) – both of which are ideal for stuffing or filling. You can choose from short pasta such as macaroni or penne or long pasta such as spaghetti or tagliatelle, all of which may be cooked and served in numerous ways.

Some pasta shapes are more suited to particular recipes than others, for example, a chunky sauce is often best served with chunky pasta or pasta shapes such as pappardelle or penne, and a smooth or thin sauce is best served with a long, fine pasta such as spaghetti or capelletti. However, there are no hard and fast rules and it is worth experimenting and choosing for yourself which pasta you prefer. Some of the varieties of pasta you will find are illustrated on page 8.

## HOME-MADE PASTA

Home-made pasta is an increasingly popular option and is relatively easy and very satisfying to make. You can make, knead, roll and shape the dough yourself or you can enlist the help of one of the many pasta-making machines available on the market. To make your own pasta you need very little equipment and once you have mastered the simple technique of making the basic pasta dough, you will find how surprisingly quick and rewarding it is to make and serve to family and friends.

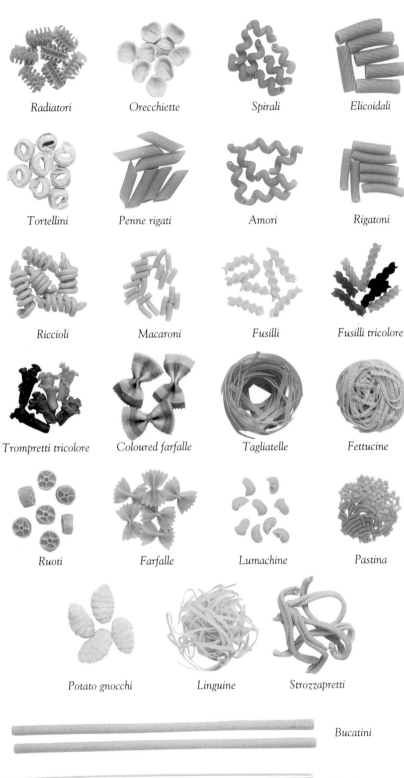

Radiatori

Orecchiette

Spirali

Elicoidali

Tortellini

Penne rigati

Amori

Rigatoni

Riccioli

Macaroni

Fusilli

Fusilli tricolore

Trompretti tricolore

Coloured farfalle

Tagliatelle

Fettucine

Ruoti

Farfalle

Lumachine

Pastina

Potato gnocchi

Linguine

Strozzapretti

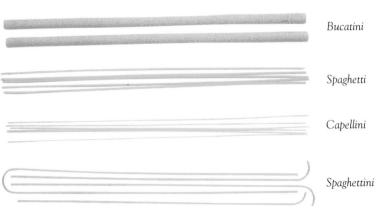

Bucatini

Spaghetti

Capellini

Spaghettini

*Cannelloni*

*Lasagne*                    *Lasagne verdi*

If you decide to make your own pasta on a regular basis, it is well worth investing in a pasta machine which will roll out and cut the dough for you. Home-made pasta can also be made with the help of a food processor or large mixer with a dough hook attachment which easily combines the ingredients to make the basic dough.

Home-made pasta is made from a simple mixture of flour, salt, eggs, oil and water. The best type of flour to use is known as 'type or grade 00' flour, but strong white flour works equally well. 'Type 00' flour is a very fine textured wheat flour and is available in many supermarkets, delicatessens or specialist Italian shops. Both 'type 00' and strong white flours have a high gluten content which makes the dough easier to knead, roll out and shape.

It really is worth experimenting and making your own pasta. Once you have mastered the basic simple techniques, you will thoroughly enjoy making and shaping the dough and you'll never taste pasta quite like it! The flavour and texture of home-made pasta readily repays the small amount of time and effort required to achieve the best results.

The following chapter in this book is devoted to making your own pasta and using the dough to make a variety of tempting plain and filled pasta dishes.

Throughout the remaining chapters of this book, a good selection of dried and fresh pasta has been used to create the wide variety of delicious pasta dishes. Dried and fresh pasta are quicker and more convenient to use than making your own pasta for each recipe and lack of time, especially when cooking a mid-week supper, is often a consideration in our hectic daily schedules. However, if you would like to use home-made pasta for these recipes, do make your own and substitute your home-made pasta for the pasta included in the recipes wherever possible. Refer to the recipes in the first chapter of this book for a general guide to the quantity of lasagne, cannelloni, etc, that the basic pasta recipe will make.

USING A PASTA MACHINE
Both electric pasta-makers and the more popular, compact, hand-turned rolling type of pasta-making machines are obtainable. Both machines come with different rollers and attachments for cutting and shaping pasta. Always read and follow the manufacturer's instructions when using a pasta machine. Most of them work in a similar way, so these basic guidelines should apply once you have made the dough and rested it (please refer to the next chapter for a basic recipe for home-made pasta).

Divide the dough into equal quantities of dough that you can easily work with – two or four pieces should suffice – and wrap all but one of the pieces in plastic wrap or cover to prevent the pasta from drying out. Press the dough out to flatten it slightly, so that it will fit through the pasta machine. Set the rollers to the widest setting and pass the dough through the rollers to make a strip of dough. Fold the dough in half, press it together and then pass it through the machine once again on the widest setting.

Repeat this procedure several more times, if necessary, to ensure the dough is smooth and of an even thickness. Then continue to pass the dough through the machine, reducing or narrowing the roller setting each time. Lightly flour the dough if it begins to feel a little sticky.

Use your hands to guide the dough through the machine but do not pull or drag the dough. Finally, pass the dough once through the machine with the rollers set on the narrowest setting. You should now have a long thin strip of pasta. Repeat this process with the remaining pieces of dough.

Place the dough over a pasta dryer (or narrow wooden pole) or on a clean tea towel and leave to dry for a few minutes, before cutting or shaping it. This relaxes the dough and helps to prevent it shrinking when cut. It also makes the pasta easier to cut and prevents the pieces of dough sticking together.

To roll out the pasta by hand, please refer to the directions given in the basic pasta recipe on page 12.

## SHAPING PASTA

To make lasagne, simply trim the edges of the pasta sheets, then cut the sheets into lengths to fit the size of your lasagne dish.

Long pasta such as tagliatelle or linguine can be cut either by hand or by using a machine. If using a machine, simply fit the appropriate cutters and pass the pasta sheets, one at a time, through the machine. Hang the noodles over a pasta dryer for a few minutes or spread them out on a clean tea towel, then gather a handful at a time and curl them into small nests before cooking.

To shape tagliatelle or linguine by hand, simply cut the dough into thin strips, or lightly flour the dough and roll up loosely into a Swiss roll, then cut into slices using a large sharp knife to the thickness required. Unroll and leave to dry for 5 minutes, then curl into nests before cooking.

Biscuit cutters and pastry wheels are useful for cutting the rolled-out dough into decorative shapes. To make filled pasta such as ravioli or tortelloni, please refer to the instructions given in the recipes on pages 14 and 20. Some pasta machines also include a ravioli filler and cutter attachment which makes the job easier.

## FLAVOURING HOME-MADE PASTA

Many different flavourings can be added to home-made pasta dough. When making the basic dough, try adding 3-4 tablespoons chopped fresh mixed herbs to the flour or a combination of herbs and crushed or finely chopped garlic (about 2 cloves) to make a tasty fresh herb or garlic and herb pasta. Add about 50g (2oz) frozen (thawed) chopped spinach to the flour for spinach pasta or pasta verde. Add 85-115g (3-4oz) finely chopped pitted black olives to the flour for olive pasta.

Experiment with other flavourings – add the finely grated rind of 2 lemons to the eggs; add 1 tablespoon white cumin seeds to the flour; add 1-2 tablespoons tomato purée, sun-dried tomato paste, curry paste or olive paste to the eggs (you may need to reduce the amount of water used slightly), etc. Try using walnut or chilli oil in place of olive oil when making the basic pasta.

Other key ingredients such as olive oil, tomatoes, onions, garlic and fresh herbs are an important feature in many pasta dishes, adding extra flavour, colour and texture and contributing to the overall appeal of the recipe.

Serve cooked plain pasta tossed with a little melted butter or olive oil and add a generous grinding of black pepper and some chopped fresh herbs, if you like. Grated fresh Parmesan cheese sprinkled on top or tossed with the pasta is another simple and delicious way of serving it.

## QUANTITIES OF PASTA

For a main meal, allow 85-115g (3-4oz) dried pasta per person or 115-150g (4-5oz) fresh pasta per person. As a general guide, 350g (12oz) dried pasta or 500g (1lb 2oz) fresh pasta, once cooked and served with a sauce or as part of a recipe, will serve 4 people for a main course. The same quantities apply to stuffed pasta such as ravioli or tortelloni.

## COOKING PASTA

Pasta should always be cooked in a large pan of lightly salted, fast-boiling water. Allow a minimum of 2 litres (70fl oz) water per 350g (12oz) pasta. You can also add a dash of olive oil to the cooking water before adding the pasta – this helps to stop the water from frothing up and over the edge of the pan and also helps to prevent the pasta sticking together. Very large saucepans, pasta pots or stockpots are the ideal vessels for cooking pasta in.

Once the water has reached a fast boil, add the pasta and stir to separate it. Return the water to a rolling boil, then calculate the cooking time from this moment. Leave the pan partially covered with the lid and stir the pasta occasionally to ensure even cooking and to prevent it sticking together.

Cooking times vary according to the type of pasta used. It is always best to follow the cooking times and guidelines on the packet. As a rough guide, dried unfilled pasta usually cooks in about 8-12 minutes and dried filled pasta in 10-15 minutes. Fresh unfilled pasta takes about 2-3 minutes to cook and fresh filled pasta about 5 minutes. The cooking time for home-made pasta is quick and is similar to that for fresh pasta.

Once cooked, pasta should be al dente (literally meaning 'to the tooth') which means the pasta should be just tender but still firm to the bite. Test the pasta frequently while it is cooking and make sure you don't overcook it.

As soon as the pasta is cooked, drain it immediately in a colander or large strainer, shake off any excess water and serve it promptly on warmed plates or in bowls. Always drain pasta thoroughly before serving. Do not rinse pasta unless you are making a recipe such as a pasta salad, where you may rinse the cooked pasta under cold running water to speed up the cooling process. Also, when pre-cooking pasta sheets or tubes such as lasagne or cannelloni, they should be rinsed under cold running water to prevent further cooking, then drained well, separated and laid out on clean tea towels ready for use.

You will find that with some pasta, such as dried cannelloni or fresh lasagne, manufacturers' cooking instructions will vary. Some manufacturers suggest pre-cooking the pasta in boiling water for 2-3 minutes, before using it in recipes, while others suggest using the pasta as it is without pre-cooking. To avoid any confusion, if you are using these types of pasta for recipes, always read and follow the basic instructions on the packet before making the recipe.

### STORING PASTA

Dried pasta, stored correctly in an airtight container in a cool, dry, dark place, will keep for up to 2 years – check the use-by date on the packet. Shop-bought fresh pasta should be kept chilled. It has a much shorter shelf-life and will keep in the refrigerator for several days, sometimes a couple of weeks, depending on the type – again, check the use-by date on the packet and do not eat the pasta beyond this date. Fresh home-made pasta should be kept chilled and used within a couple of days of making.

Uncooked fresh pasta freezes well and can be cooked from frozen, allowing nominal extra cooking time. Plain cooked pasta does not freeze very well, but dishes such as macaroni cheese where the pasta is coated with a fairly thick sauce tend to freeze quite well. Baked dishes containing pasta such as lasagne or cannelloni also freeze well.

# BASIC EGG PASTA

225g (8oz) 'type 00' flour or strong white flour
½ teaspoon salt
2 eggs
1 tablespoon olive oil
1-2 tablespoons cold water

Sift flour and salt into a mound on a clean work surface. Make a well in the centre and add eggs, oil and 1 tablespoon water.

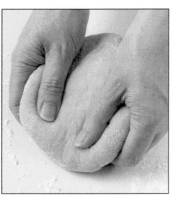

Using your fingers, gradually work all the dry ingredients into egg mixture, adding a little extra water if necessary to make a soft but not sticky dough. Knead dough on a lightly floured surface for 5-10 minutes or until smooth and elastic. Form dough into a ball, place in a polythene bag and leave to rest at room temperature for 30 minutes, before shaping as required.

Use a pasta machine to roll and cut the dough (see page 9) or, alternatively, roll out the dough on a lightly floured surface as thinly as possible. Using a sharp knife, cut the pasta into the shapes required. For lasagne, simply cut the pasta into rectangular or square sheets to fit the size of your lasagne dish.

To make tagliatelle, either use a pasta machine to roll the dough, allow it to dry for a few minutes, and then feed the pasta sheets through the machine fitted with the correct cutters. Alternatively, cut the dough into thin strips, or lightly flour the dough and roll up loosely into a Swiss roll. Cut into slices to the thickness required. Unroll and leave to dry for 5 minutes before cooking. Home-made pasta should be left to dry for 5-10 minutes before cooking. Spread it out on a clean tea towel or hang it over a pasta dryer or wooden pole to dry out.

Fresh pasta only takes a few minutes to cook; for example, fresh tagliatelle or spaghetti will only take 2-3 minutes to cook. Cook pasta in plenty of lightly salted, fast-boiling water in a large saucepan or pasta pan. Partially cover the pan and give the pasta an occasional stir during cooking. When it is cooked, the pasta will rise to the top of the cooking liquid. Drain thoroughly and serve immediately.

Home-made pasta can also be made using a food processor. Simply sift the flour and salt into the food processor bowl, then add the eggs, oil and 1 tablespoon water. Process until the dough just begins to come together, adding a little extra water if necessary, to form a soft but not sticky dough. Gather the dough together, wrap and rest as above.

## —— THREE CHEESE RAVIOLI ——

1 quantity Basic Egg Pasta dough (see page 12)
115g (4oz) ricotta cheese
100g (3½oz) pecorino cheese, finely grated
50g (2oz) fresh Parmesan cheese, finely grated, plus
  extra, to serve
1 large egg, beaten
freshly ground black pepper
extra beaten egg, for brushing
50g (2oz) butter, melted, to serve
flat-leaf parsley sprigs, to garnish

Make the pasta dough as described on page 12 and leave to rest for 30 minutes.

Put ricotta, pecorino and Parmesan cheeses in a bowl with egg and black pepper and mix well. Divide pasta dough in half and roll out each piece of dough as thinly as possible on a lightly floured surface. Cut each pasta sheet into 5cm (2in) rounds using a biscuit cutter. Spoon small mounds of cheese filling into the centre of the rounds, brush edges with beaten egg, then fold dough over filling to make a semi-circle. Press edges firmly together to seal.

Transfer to a lightly floured tea towel and leave to rest and dry out for 20 minutes. Bring a large saucepan of lightly salted water to the boil. Add ravioli and cook for 3-5 minutes, or until ravioli is tender and rises to the surface. Drain well and toss with melted butter and extra freshly ground black pepper. Sprinkle with Parmesan cheese and serve garnished with parsley sprigs. Serve with a mixed baby leaf salad.

*Serves 4*

# SPICY BEEF RAVIOLI

1 quantity Basic Egg Pasta dough (see page 12)
1 tablespoon olive oil, plus extra to serve
1 shallot, finely chopped
1 small fresh red chilli, seeded and finely chopped
1 clove garlic, crushed
1 teaspoon ground coriander
1 teaspoon ground cumin
115g (4oz) cooked beef, minced
50g (2oz) prosciutto, finely chopped
1 tablespoon tomato purée
1 egg, beaten
2 tablespoons fresh breadcrumbs
salt and freshly ground black pepper
herb sprigs, to garnish

Make pasta dough as described on page 12 and leave to rest for 30 minutes. Heat oil in a saucepan, add shallot, chilli and garlic and cook gently for 5 minutes, stirring occasionally. Add ground spices and cook for 1 minute, stirring. Add beef and cook gently for 2 minutes, stirring. Remove pan from heat, add prosciutto, tomato purée, egg, breadcrumbs and salt and pepper and mix well. Divide pasta dough in half and roll out each piece of dough as thinly as possible on a lightly floured surface to form a large square.

Cut each sheet into 5cm (2in) squares using a knife or pastry wheel. Spoon small mounds of beef filling on to squares, dampen edges, then fold to make a triangle. Press edges firmly together to seal. Transfer to a lightly floured tea towel and leave to rest for 20 minutes. Bring a large saucepan of lightly salted water to the boil. Cook ravioli for 3-5 minutes, or until ravioli is tender and rises to the surface. Drain well and toss with a little olive oil and black pepper. Garnish with herb sprigs.

*Serves 4*

# — BEEF & MUSHROOM LASAGNE —

1 quantity Basic Egg Pasta dough (see page 12)
1 tablespoon olive oil
2 red onions, chopped
2 cloves garlic, crushed
500g (1lb 2oz) lean minced beef
350g (12oz) mushrooms, sliced
500ml (18fl oz) passata
2 tablespoons tomato purée
2 tablespoons chopped fresh mixed herbs
salt and freshly ground black pepper
500g (1lb 2oz) fresh spinach leaves, washed
40g (1½oz) butter
40g (1½oz) plain flour
550ml (20fl oz) milk
115g (4oz) pecorino cheese, grated
25g (1oz) fresh Parmesan cheese, finely grated

Make pasta dough as described on page 12. Leave to rest for 30 minutes. Meanwhile, make filling. Heat oil in a saucepan, add onions and garlic and cook for 3 minutes, stirring occasionally. Add beef and cook until browned all over. Add mushrooms, passata, tomato purée, herbs and salt and pepper and mix well. Bring to boil, cover and simmer for 30 minutes, stirring occasionally. Uncover, increase the heat slightly and cook for a further 10-15 minutes to thicken the sauce slightly.

Preheat the oven to 190C (375F/Gas 5). Lightly grease an ovenproof lasagne dish or baking tin. Put spinach in a large saucepan with just the water that clings to its leaves. Cover and cook for 3-4 minutes, or until just wilted. Drain well and press out excess water. Chop and season with salt and pepper.

Put butter, flour and milk in a saucepan. Heat gently, whisking continuously, until sauce is thickened and smooth. Simmer for 3 minutes, stirring. Remove pan from heat, whisk in pecorino cheese and season to taste. Cover sauce closely with greaseproof paper and set aside. Roll out pasta dough thinly on a lightly floured surface. Cut into 9 rectangles each about 15x10cm (6x4in).

Cook lasagne sheets in batches in a large pan of lightly salted boiling water for 2 minutes. Drain, refresh under cold running water, then drain again on paper towels. Spoon one-third of meat sauce into prepared dish, then top with one-third of spinach. Top this with 3 sheets of lasagne.

Continue layering in this way ending with a layer of lasagne. Pour cheese sauce evenly over lasagne. Sprinkle with Parmesan. Bake for 35-40 minutes until golden and bubbling. Serve with hot garlic bread and a side salad.

*Serves 4-6*

VARIATIONS: Use lean minced lamb or pork in place of beef. Use sliced courgettes in place of mushrooms.

# — MUSHROOM CANNELLONI —

1 quantity Basic Egg Pasta dough (see page 12)
40g (1½oz) butter
1 tablespoon olive oil
1 leek, washed and finely chopped
225g (8oz) chestnut mushrooms, finely chopped
1 courgette, finely chopped
200g (7oz) Cheddar or pecorino cheese, grated
1 egg, beaten
1 teaspoon mushroom ketchup
1 tablespoon chopped fresh parsley
1 teaspoon chopped fresh tarragon
salt and freshly ground black pepper
15g (½oz) plain flour
300ml (10fl oz) milk
herb sprigs, to garnish

Make pasta dough as described on page 12 and leave to rest for 30 minutes. Preheat the oven to 180C (350F/Gas 4). Lightly grease a shallow ovenproof dish or baking pan. Meanwhile, make filling. Heat 25g (1oz) butter and the oil in a pan until butter has melted. Add leek, mushrooms and courgette and cook over a fairly high heat for 5 minutes, stirring occasionally.

Remove pan from heat, cool slightly, then drain off any excess liquid. Add 85g (3oz) Cheddar or pecorino, the egg, ketchup, chopped herbs and salt and pepper and mix well. Set aside. Make cheese sauce. Melt remaining butter in a pan, add flour and cook gently for 1 minute, stirring.

Gradually whisk in milk, then heat gently, whisking continuously, until sauce is thickened and smooth. Simmer gently for 2 minutes, stirring. Remove pan from heat, stir in half remaining cheese, season with salt and pepper, cover closely with greaseproof paper and set aside.

Roll out pasta dough very thinly on lightly floured surface and cut into 12 even rectangles, each about 15x10cm (6x4in). Cook pasta sheets in batches in a large pan of lightly salted boiling water for 3 minutes. Remove from pan using a slotted spoon, refresh under cold running water, then drain on paper towels. Spoon mushroom filling mixture along width of each pasta sheet, then roll them up to make filled cannelloni tubes.

Arrange filled tubes, seam-side down, in prepared dish. Pour sauce over and sprinkle with remaining cheese. Bake for 35-40 minutes, or until golden and bubbling. Garnish with herb sprigs and serve with crusty French bread.

*Serves 4*

VARIATIONS: Use fresh wild mushrooms in place of chestnut mushrooms. Use chopped fresh sage or rosemary in place of tarragon.

# — HAM & CHEESE TORTELLONI —

1 quantity Basic Egg Pasta dough (see page 12)
115g (4oz) lean smoked ham, finely chopped
25g (1oz) Parma ham, finely chopped
50g (2oz) ricotta cheese
25g (1oz) fresh Parmesan cheese, finely grated
1 egg
salt and freshly ground black pepper
50g (2oz) butter, diced, to serve
chopped fresh flat-leaf parsley, to garnish

Make pasta dough as described on page 12 and leave to rest for 30 minutes. Make the filling. Put both hams, ricotta and Parmesan cheeses, egg and salt and pepper in a bowl and mix thoroughly. Set aside.

Divide pasta dough in half and roll out each piece of dough very thinly on a lightly floured surface. Cut dough into rounds using a 5cm (2in) cutter. Spoon a little filling on to each dough round, brush the edges with a little water and fold over to make a semi-circle, pressing the edges firmly together to seal. Wrap each filled pasta shape around your little finger and cross the ends over, pinching them together. Slide off your finger on to a floured surface and leave to dry for 20 minutes.

Cook pasta in a large saucepan of lightly salted boiling water for 3-5 minutes, or until tender. Drain thoroughly in a colander, then return to the rinsed-out pan. Add diced butter and freshly ground black pepper and toss to coat all over. Sprinkle with chopped parsley to garnish, then serve with warm ciabatta bread.

*Serves 4*

VARIATION: Use finely grated pecorino or Cheddar cheese in place of ricotta cheese.

# — POTATO & HERB GNOCCHI —

700g (1½lb) peeled potatoes, diced
40g (1½oz) fresh Parmesan cheese, finely grated,
  plus extra to serve
85g (3oz) butter
1 egg, beaten
1 tablespoon chopped fresh flat-leaf parsley
1 tablespoon chopped fresh basil
1 tablespoon chopped fresh oregano or marjoram
salt and freshly ground black pepper
200g (7oz) plain flour
1-2 cloves garlic, crushed
herb sprigs, to garnish

Cook potatoes in a saucepan of boiling water for 10-15 minutes, or until tender.

Drain well, then return to the pan and mash until smooth. Add Parmesan cheese, 25g (1oz) butter, the egg, chopped herbs and salt and pepper and beat until smooth and well mixed. Add half the flour and mix well, then gradually add remaining flour, mixing until dough is smooth, even and slightly sticky. Shape dough into small balls and press a fork into top surface of each ball to flatten slightly and leave an impression.

Place gnocchi on a lightly floured plate and chill for 30 minutes. Cook in batches in a large saucepan of lightly salted boiling water for 4-5 minutes. Remove from pan using a slotted spoon, drain well and keep hot. Melt remaining butter in a saucepan, add garlic and cook gently for 2 minutes, stirring. Pour butter over gnocchi and toss to coat. Sprinkle with grated Parmesan cheese, garnish with herb sprigs and serve with a mixed green salad.

*Serves 4-6*

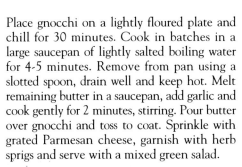

# TOMATO & LENTIL SOUP

115g (4oz) dried green or brown lentils
1 bay leaf
1 tablespoon olive oil
1 large red onion, chopped
1 clove garlic, crushed
1kg (2¼lb) plum tomatoes, chopped
1 tablespoon sun-dried tomato paste
850ml (30fl oz) vegetable stock
½ teaspoon caster sugar
salt and freshly ground black pepper
50g (2oz) dried mini pasta shapes such as
   conchigliette rigate
3 tablespoons chopped fresh flat-leaf parsley
a little crème fraîche and herb sprigs, to garnish

Cook lentils in a large saucepan of boiling water with bay leaf for 30-40 minutes, or until tender. Rinse, drain and set aside. Discard bay leaf. Heat oil in a large saucepan, add onion and garlic and cook for 5 minutes, stirring occasionally, until softened. Stir in tomatoes, tomato paste, stock, sugar and salt and pepper. Bring to the boil, then reduce the heat, cover and simmer for 25 minutes, stirring occasionally. Remove pan from the heat and cool slightly.

Purée soup in a blender or food processor until smooth, then pass mixture through a sieve into rinsed-out pan. Discard contents of sieve. Stir pasta into soup and bring gently to the boil. Cover and simmer for 10-15 minutes, stirring occasionally, until pasta is cooked. Stir in lentils and chopped parsley and reheat gently until hot. Ladle into warmed soup bowls to serve. Garnish with a swirl of crème fraîche and herb sprigs. Serve with crusty fresh bread.

*Serves 4*

# – ROAST TOMATO PASTA SOUP –

900g (2lb) tomatoes, cut in half
3 tablespoons olive oil
2 onions, chopped
2 cloves garlic, finely chopped
1 litre (35fl oz) vegetable stock
1 tablespoon tomato purée
salt and freshly ground black pepper
100g (3½oz) dried tubettini or mini macaroni
8 small slices of French stick
50g (2oz) Gruyère cheese, finely grated
3 tablespoons chopped fresh basil
basil sprigs, to garnish

Preheat oven to 180C (350F/Gas 4). Put tomatoes in a single layer, cut-side-up, in an ovenproof dish. Drizzle with 2 tablespoons of the oil. Roast for 40 minutes or until soft. Set aside. Heat remaining oil in a saucepan, add onions and garlic and sauté for 5 minutes or until soft. Stir in tomatoes, stock, tomato purée and salt and pepper. Bring to the boil, reduce heat, cover and simmer for 20 minutes, stirring occasionally. Cool slightly. Purée soup in a blender or food processor, then pass through a sieve into rinsed-out pan. Discard contents of sieve.

Add pasta to soup and bring gently to the boil. Cover and simmer for 10-15 minutes, stirring occasionally, until pasta is cooked. Meanwhile, make croutons. Preheat grill to high. Toast bread slices on one side, then turn them over and top each one with some grated Gruyère. Grill until cheese is melted and bubbling. Stir chopped basil into soup, then ladle into warmed soup bowls. Serve topped with hot Gruyère croutons and garnish with basil sprigs.

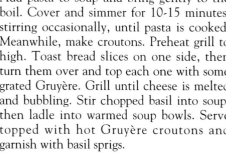

Serves 4

# PASTA & BEAN SOUP

1 tablespoon olive oil
2 leeks, washed and sliced
2 sticks celery, chopped
2 carrots, thinly sliced
225g (8oz) swede, diced
1 bulb fennel, diced
400g (14oz) can chopped tomatoes
1.4 litres (50fl oz) vegetable stock
salt and freshly ground black pepper
400g (14oz) can flageolet or borlotti beans, rinsed
   and drained
115g (4oz) dried lumachine
2-3 tablespoons chopped fresh coriander
coriander sprigs, to garnish

Heat oil in a large saucepan, add leeks and celery and cook gently for 5 minutes, stirring occasionally. Add carrots, swede, fennel, tomatoes, stock and salt and pepper and stir to mix. Bring to the boil, then reduce heat, cover and simmer for 20 minutes, stirring occasionally.

Stir in beans and pasta and return to the boil. Cover and simmer for a further 10-15 minutes, stirring occasionally, until pasta is cooked. Stir in chopped coriander and ladle into warmed soup bowls to serve. Garnish with coriander sprigs and serve with fresh bread rolls.

*Serves 4-6*

VARIATIONS: Use turnip, celeriac or parsnips in place of swede. Use chopped fresh parsley or basil in place of coriander.

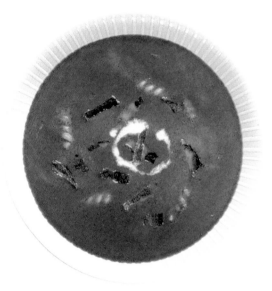

# — SPINACH & STILTON SOUP —

25g (1oz) butter
1 onion, chopped
3 sticks celery, finely chopped
850ml (30fl oz) vegetable stock
300ml (10fl oz) milk
salt and freshly ground black pepper
450g (1lb) fresh spinach, washed and shredded
85g (3oz) dried mini pasta shapes such as fusillini
4 rashers rindless smoked streaky bacon
150g (5oz) Stilton cheese, crumbled

Melt butter in a large saucepan, add onion and celery and cook for 8 minutes, stirring occasionally.

Stir in stock, milk and salt and pepper. Bring to the boil, then reduce heat, cover and simmer for 10 minutes, stirring occasionally. Add spinach and simmer gently for 10 minutes or until spinach is tender. Remove pan from heat and cool slightly, then purée in a blender or food processor until smooth. Return soup to rinsed-out pan, add pasta, bring to boil and simmer for a further 10-15 minutes, stirring occasionally, until pasta is cooked.

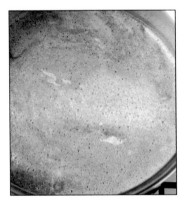

Meanwhile, preheat grill to high. Grill bacon for 3-4 minutes, turning once, until crisp. Drain on paper towels and set aside. Stir Stilton into soup and heat gently until cheese has melted and soup is hot. Ladle into warmed soup bowls. Chop or crumble bacon and sprinkle over soup. Serve with crusty fresh bread.

*Serves 4-6*

VARIATION: Use other blue cheese such as Gorgonzola in place of Stilton.

## CHICKEN PASTA SOUP

500g (1lb 2oz) skinless chicken thigh fillets
1 onion, chopped
1 clove garlic, crushed
2 sticks celery, chopped
2 carrots, thinly sliced
salt and freshly ground black pepper
2 leeks, washed and thinly sliced
115g (4oz) quick-cook dried macaroni
4 tablespoons crème fraîche (optional)
2 tablespoons chopped fresh parsley
parsley sprigs, to garnish

Put chicken thigh fillets, onion, garlic, celery, carrots and salt and pepper in a large saucepan and add 1.2 litres (40fl oz) water.

Bring to the boil and remove and discard any scum that rises to the surface. Reduce heat, cover and simmer for 45 minutes. Lift out chicken using a slotted spoon and break into smaller pieces, then return chicken to soup.

Stir in leeks and pasta and return to the boil. Cover and simmer for a further 10-15 minutes, stirring occasionally, until pasta is cooked. Stir in crème fraîche, if using, and chopped parsley, then ladle into warmed soup bowls. Garnish with parsley sprigs and serve with fresh soft bread rolls.

*Serves 4-6*

VARIATION: Use chopped fresh coriander in place of parsley.

# MINESTRONE

2 tablespoons olive oil
1 onion, finely chopped
1 clove garlic, crushed
2 sticks celery, finely chopped
2 carrots, finely diced
1 leek, washed and sliced
50g (2oz) rindless streaky bacon rashers, chopped
1.3 litres (45fl oz) vegetable or beef stock
400g (14oz) can chopped tomatoes
1 tablespoon tomato purée
2 teaspoons dried herbes de Provence
400g (14oz) can borlotti beans, rinsed and drained
50g (2oz) small dried pasta shapes such as tubettini
  or farfalline
salt and freshly ground black pepper
freshly grated Parmesan cheese, to serve

Heat oil in a large saucepan, add onion and garlic and cook gently for 5 minutes, stirring occasionally. Add celery, carrots, leek and bacon and cook for a further 5 minutes.

Stir in stock, tomatoes, tomato purée, herbs, beans, pasta and salt and pepper. Bring to the boil, then reduce heat, cover and simmer for 25-30 minutes, stirring occasionally, until pasta and vegetables are cooked. Ladle into warmed soup bowls and sprinkle with freshly grated Parmesan cheese. Serve with warm ciabatta bread.

*Serves 4-6*

VARIATION: Use cannellini beans in place of borlotti beans.

## SPICY SAUSAGE SOUP

1 tablespoon olive oil
1 large onion, thinly sliced
1 clove garlic, crushed
2 courgettes, diced
175g (6oz) cooked chorizo sausage, thinly sliced
85g (3oz) dried pastina (tiny soup pasta)
  or mennucci (little stars)
1 litre (35fl oz) vegetable stock
1 tablespoon tomato purée
salt and freshly ground black pepper
2-3 tablespoons chopped fresh flat-leaf parsley
crisp croutons and fresh Parmesan cheese shavings,
  to serve

Heat oil in a large saucepan, add onion and garlic and cook gently for 10 minutes, stirring occasionally, until softened. Stir in courgettes, chorizo, pasta, stock, tomato purée and salt and pepper. Bring to the boil, then reduce heat, cover and simmer for 10-15 minutes, stirring occasionally, until vegetables and pasta are cooked.

Stir in the parsley and ladle into warmed soup bowls. Sprinkle with crisp croutons and shavings of Parmesan cheese, just before serving. Serve with crusty French bread.

*Serves 4*

VARIATION: Use 300g (10oz) sliced chestnut mushrooms or button mushrooms in place of courgettes.

# — BEEF BROTH WITH SHALLOTS —

1 tablespoon sunflower oil
8 shallots, thinly sliced
175g (6oz) button mushrooms, sliced
1.2 litres (40fl oz) good home-made beef stock
salt and freshly ground black pepper
115g (4oz) dried lumachine
1 tablespoon chopped fresh parsley
1 tablespoon chopped fresh marjoram or oregano
herb sprigs, to garnish

Heat oil in a large saucepan, add the shallots and cook gently for 5 minutes, stirring occasionally.

Add mushrooms and cook for a further 2 minutes. Stir in stock and salt and pepper. Bring to the boil, then reduce heat, cover and simmer for 10 minutes, stirring occasionally.

Stir in pasta, cover and simmer for a further 10-15 minutes, stirring occasionally, until vegetables and pasta are cooked. Stir in chopped herbs, then ladle into warmed soup bowls. Garnish with herb sprigs and serve with soft bread rolls.

*Serves 4*

VARIATION: Use 1 large onion, finely chopped, in place of shallots.

# CREAMY MUSSEL SOUP

2kg (4½lb) fresh mussels in shells, cleaned
550ml (20fl oz) fish or vegetable stock
100ml (3½fl oz) dry white wine
1 small onion, cut into quarters
1 bouquet garni
25g (1oz) butter
2 leeks, washed and thinly sliced
2 sticks celery, finely chopped
85g (3oz) dried conchigliette
salt and freshly ground black pepper
150ml (5fl oz) double cream
1 tablespoon chopped fresh parsley
1 tablespoon chopped fresh dill

Put mussels in a large saucepan with stock, wine, onion and bouquet garni. Cover, bring to the boil and cook for 4-5 minutes, shaking pan occasionally, until mussels open. Strain mussels, reserving liquid and mussels separately. Discard any mussels whose shells have not opened. Discard onion and bouquet garni. Remove most of mussels from their shells, but reserve a few for garnish. Set aside. Melt butter in a clean saucepan, add leeks and celery and cook gently for 5 minutes, stirring occasionally, until softened.

Stir in reserved strained stock, pasta and salt and pepper. Bring to the boil, then reduce heat, cover and simmer for 10-15 minutes, stirring occasionally, until pasta is cooked. Stir in shelled mussels, cream and chopped herbs and heat gently until hot, stirring. Ladle into warmed soup bowls and garnish with reserved mussels in their shells. Serve with warm crusty bread.

*Serves 4-6*

# SPAGHETTI BOLOGNESE

1 tablespoon olive oil
2 onions, chopped
1 carrot, finely chopped
2 sticks celery, finely chopped
1 clove garlic, crushed
500g (1lb 2oz) lean minced beef
1 tablespoon plain flour
225g (8oz) chestnut mushrooms, sliced
400g (14oz) can chopped tomatoes
1 tablespoon tomato purée
300ml (10fl oz) beef or vegetable stock
300ml (10fl oz) red wine
2 teaspoons dried Italian herb seasoning
salt and freshly ground black pepper
350g (12oz) dried spaghetti
freshly grated Parmesan cheese, to serve

Heat oil in a large saucepan, add onions, carrot, celery and garlic and cook for 5 minutes, stirring occasionally. Add minced beef and cook, stirring occasionally, until meat is browned all over. Add flour and cook for 1 minute, stirring. Add mushrooms, tomatoes, tomato purée, stock, wine, herbs and salt and pepper and stir to mix. Bring to the boil, then reduce heat, cover and simmer for about 1 hour, stirring occasionally, until meat is cooked and sauce is well reduced.

Cook pasta in a large saucepan of lightly salted boiling water for 10-12 minutes, or until just cooked or al dente. Drain thoroughly and divide between warmed serving plates. Spoon the meat sauce over the pasta, sprinkle with Parmesan cheese and serve with hot garlic bread.

*Serves 4-6*

COOK'S TIP: To thicken meat sauce, uncover pan and increase heat slightly 15-20 minutes before the end of cooking time.

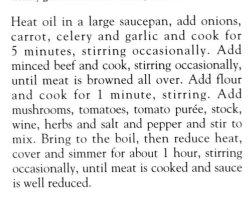

# — HAM & GORGONZOLA SAUCE —

2 tablespoons olive oil
1 leek, washed and sliced
225g (8oz) button mushrooms, sliced
1 clove garlic, crushed
2 tablespoons dry sherry
150ml (5fl oz) double cream
salt and freshly ground black pepper
115g (4oz) lean smoked ham, diced
115g (4oz) Gorgonzola cheese, diced
2 tablespoons chopped fresh parsley
500g (1lb 2oz) fresh tagliatelle
herb sprigs, to garnish

Heat oil in a frying pan, add leek, mushrooms and garlic, and sauté for 8-10 minutes.

Add sherry and cook over a fairly high heat, stirring frequently, until most of liquid has evaporated. Reduce heat, stir in cream and salt and pepper and cook gently for 1-2 minutes. Stir in ham, cheese and chopped parsley and heat gently until hot, stirring.

Meanwhile, cook pasta in a large saucepan of lightly salted boiling water for 3 minutes, or until just cooked or al dente. Drain thoroughly and return to rinsed-out pan. Add ham and cheese sauce to pasta and toss well to mix. Serve on warmed plates and garnish with herb sprigs. Serve with a green salad.

*Serves 4*

VARIATION: Use lean smoked chicken or turkey in place of ham.

# – FRAZZLED PROSCIUTTO SAUCE –

2 tablespoons olive oil
12 thin slices of prosciutto, about 175g (6oz)
4 shallots, finely chopped
2 courgettes, finely chopped
1 tablespoon chopped fresh flat-leaf parsley
1 tablespoon chopped fresh basil
1 tablespoon chopped fresh oregano or marjoram
300g (10oz) crème fraîche
salt and freshly ground black pepper
500g (1lb 2oz) fresh fusilli
herb sprigs, to garnish

Heat 1 tablespoon oil in a non-stick frying pan, cook prosciutto over a fairly high heat, turning frequently, until crinkled and crisp.

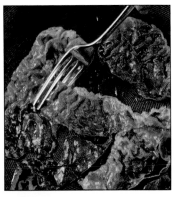

Transfer to a plate, set aside and keep hot. Add remaining oil to frying pan and heat until hot, then add shallots and cook for 3 minutes, stirring occasionally. Add courgettes and cook for a further 7 minutes, stirring frequently, until vegetables are just cooked. Stir in chopped herbs, crème fraîche and salt and pepper and heat gently until hot, stirring.

Meanwhile, cook pasta in a large saucepan of lightly salted boiling water for 3 minutes, or until just cooked or al dente. Drain thoroughly and return to rinsed-out pan. Snip frazzled prosciutto into thin strips or pieces and stir into herb sauce. Pour sauce over pasta and toss well to mix. Serve on warmed plates and garnish with herb sprigs. Serve with a mixed leaf salad.

*Serves 4*

# — SWEET & SOUR PORK SAUCE —

350g (12oz) dried fettuccine
salt and freshly ground black pepper
2 tablespoons sunflower oil
2 courgettes, thinly sliced
1 red pepper, seeded and sliced
1 bunch spring onions, chopped
1 clove garlic, crushed
450g (1lb) lean pork fillet, cut into thin strips
1 tablespoon cornflour
100ml (3½fl oz) apple juice
100ml (3½fl oz) vegetable stock
2 tablespoons light soy sauce
2 tablespoons dry sherry
2 tablespoons red wine vinegar
2 tablespoons runny honey
2 tablespoons tomato ketchup

Cook pasta in a large saucepan of lightly salted boiling water for 10-12 minutes, or until just cooked or al dente. Meanwhile, heat oil in a wok or large frying pan, add courgettes, red pepper, spring onions and garlic and stir-fry over a fairly high heat for 3 minutes. Add pork and stir-fry for about 5 minutes, or until cooked.

Blend cornflour with apple juice and add to the wok together with stock, soy sauce, sherry, vinegar, honey, tomato ketchup and salt and pepper. Stir-fry until sauce comes to the boil and thickens, then simmer for 2-3 minutes, stirring frequently. Drain pasta and serve on warmed plates. Spoon pork sauce over pasta and serve.

*Serves 4*

VARIATION: Use lean beef or chicken breast in place of pork.

# — HERBY SAUSAGE & GARLIC —

25g (1oz) butter
1 tablespoon olive oil
1 red onion, finely chopped
2 cloves garlic, finely chopped
1 x 400g (14oz) can AND 1 x 225g (8oz) can
   chopped tomatoes
100ml (3½fl oz) red wine
salt and freshly ground black pepper
12 thin Cumberland or other herby sausages, about
   350g (12oz)
350g (12oz) dried wholewheat fusilli pasta
1 tablespoon chopped fresh parsley
1 tablespoon chopped fresh oregano
25-50g (1-2oz) freshly shaved Parmesan,
   to garnish

Heat butter and oil in a saucepan until butter has melted. Add onion and garlic and cook gently for 5 minutes, stirring occasionally. Stir in tomatoes, wine and salt and pepper and bring to the boil. Cook, uncovered, over a moderate heat for 20-25 minutes, stirring occasionally, until sauce is thick and pulpy. Meanwhile, preheat grill to high. Grill sausages for about 15 minutes, turning occasionally, until thoroughly cooked, brown and crisp on the outside. Cut sausages into slices.

In the meantime, cook pasta in a large saucepan of lightly salted boiling water for 10 minutes, or until just cooked or al dente. Drain thoroughly and return to rinsed-out pan. Add sausage slices and chopped herbs to tomato sauce and stir well. Pour over pasta and toss well to mix. Serve on warmed plates and sprinkle with shavings of Parmesan cheese to garnish. Serve with warm ciabatta bread.

*Serves 4-6*

# — BRANDIED CHICKEN LIVERS —

25g (1oz) butter
1 tablespoon sunflower oil
4 shallots, thinly sliced
1 clove garlic, crushed
400g (14oz) chicken livers, chopped
175g (6oz) mushrooms, sliced
100ml (3½fl oz) brandy
4 tablespoons crème fraîche
1 tablespoon chopped fresh parsley
1 tablespoon chopped fresh marjoram or oregano
salt and freshly ground black pepper
500g (1lb 2oz) fresh garlic and herb tagliatelle
herb sprigs, to garnish

Heat butter and oil in a large frying pan until butter has melted.

Add shallots and garlic and cook for 5 minutes, stirring occasionally. Add chicken livers and mushrooms and cook over a fairly high heat, stirring frequently, until chicken livers are sealed and browned all over. Stir in brandy and cook over a high heat for 3-5 minutes, stirring frequently, until liquid has reduced by about half. Reduce heat, stir in the crème fraîche, chopped herbs and salt and pepper and heat gently until hot.

Meanwhile, cook pasta in a large saucepan of lightly salted boiling water for 3 minutes, or until just cooked or al dente. Drain thoroughly. Serve pasta on warmed plates and spoon sauce over the top. Garnish with herb sprigs and serve with a mixed baby leaf salad.

*Serves 4*

VARIATION: Use sliced courgettes in place of mushrooms.

# — SMOKED TROUT & ALMONDS —

2 tablespoons sunflower oil
2 leeks, washed and thinly sliced
2 courgettes, thinly sliced
25g (1oz) butter
25g (1oz) plain flour
450ml (16fl oz) fish or vegetable stock
150ml (5fl oz) dry white wine
225g (8oz) skinless smoked trout fillets, chopped
2-3 teaspoons chopped fresh tarragon
salt and freshly ground black pepper
500g (1lb 2oz) fresh spaghetti
50g (2oz) toasted flaked almonds

Heat oil in a frying pan, add leeks and
courgettes and cook gently for 8-10 minutes,
stirring occasionally, until softened.

Meanwhile, melt butter in a saucepan, add
flour and cook gently for 1 minute, stirring.
Gradually whisk in stock and wine, then
heat gently, whisking continuously, until
sauce is thickened and smooth. Simmer
gently for 2 minutes, stirring.

Stir leek mixture, smoked trout, tarragon
and salt and pepper into sauce and heat
gently, stirring occasionally, until piping
hot. In the meantime, cook pasta in a large
saucepan of lightly salted boiling water for
3 minutes, or until just cooked or al dente.
Drain thoroughly and return to the rinsed-
out pan. Add trout sauce and almonds to
pasta and toss well to mix. Serve with soft
bread rolls.

Serves 4-6

# — TUNA & PEPPERCORN SAUCE —

50g (2oz) butter
6 shallots, finely chopped
175g (6oz) chestnut mushrooms, sliced
40g (1½oz) plain flour
500ml (18fl oz) milk
50g (2oz) Cheddar cheese, grated
400g (14oz) can tuna in brine, drained and flaked
1 tablespoon green peppercorns in brine, drained
2 tablespoons chopped fresh flat-leaf parsley
salt and freshly ground black pepper
500g (1lb 2oz) fresh fettuccine
parsley sprigs, to garnish

Melt 15g (½oz) butter in a saucepan, add shallots and mushrooms and sauté gently for about 10 minutes, until softened.

Meanwhile, put remaining butter in a separate saucepan with flour and milk. Heat gently, whisking continuously, until sauce is thickened and smooth. Simmer gently for 3 minutes, stirring. Remove pan from heat and stir in cheese until melted, then stir in shallots, mushrooms, tuna, peppercorns, chopped parsley and salt and pepper. Heat gently until hot, stirring occasionally.

In the meantime, cook pasta in a large saucepan of lightly salted boiling water for 3 minutes, or until just cooked or al dente. Drain thoroughly and return to the rinsed-out saucepan. Add fish sauce to pasta and toss well to mix. Serve on warmed plates and garnish with parsley sprigs. Serve with fresh crusty bread.

*Serves 4*

VARIATION: Use canned salmon in place of tuna.

# SPICY PRAWN & TOMATO SAUCE

175g (6oz) small broccoli florets
40g (1½oz) butter
1 leek, washed and sliced
2 cloves garlic, crushed
1½ teaspoons hot chilli powder
1 teaspoon ground coriander
1 teaspoon ground cumin
175g (6oz) button mushrooms, sliced
150ml (5fl oz) dry white wine
400g (14oz) can chopped tomatoes
salt and freshly ground black pepper
350g (12oz) cooked, peeled king prawns
350g (12oz) dried penne
2 tablespoons chopped fresh coriander

Cook broccoli in a saucepan of boiling water for 5 minutes, or until just tender. Drain well and set aside. Melt butter in a large saucepan, add leek and garlic and cook gently for 5 minutes, stirring occasionally. Add ground spices and cook for 1 minute, stirring. Add mushrooms, wine, tomatoes and salt and pepper and stir to mix. Bring to the boil, then reduce heat, cover and simmer for 10 minutes, stirring occasionally. Uncover pan, increase heat and cook for a further 10 minutes, stirring occasionally, until sauce has thickened slightly.

Stir in broccoli and prawns and cook for 5 minutes or until piping hot. Meanwhile, cook pasta in a large saucepan of lightly salted boiling water for 10 minutes, or until just cooked or al dente. Drain thoroughly and serve on warmed plates. Stir chopped coriander into tomato sauce, then spoon sauce over pasta. Serve with crusty fresh bread.

*Serves 4*

# CLAM & SWEETCORN CAPELLINI

1kg (2¼lb) fresh clams in their shells, cleaned
4 tablespoons dry white wine
15g (½oz) butter
1 tablespoon olive oil
2 leeks, washed and sliced
1 clove garlic, crushed
200g (7oz) can sweetcorn kernels, drained
225g (8oz) frozen petit pois, thawed
300ml (10fl oz) double cream
salt and freshly ground black pepper
2 tablespoons chopped fresh flat-leaf parsley
500g (1lb 2oz) fresh capellini

Put clams in a large saucepan with wine. Cover and cook for 5-7 minutes, shaking pan occasionally, until clams have opened.

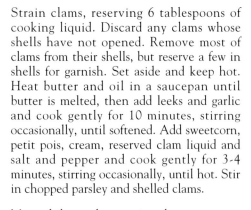

Strain clams, reserving 6 tablespoons of cooking liquid. Discard any clams whose shells have not opened. Remove most of clams from their shells, but reserve a few in shells for garnish. Set aside and keep hot. Heat butter and oil in a saucepan until butter is melted, then add leeks and garlic and cook gently for 10 minutes, stirring occasionally, until softened. Add sweetcorn, petit pois, cream, reserved clam liquid and salt and pepper and cook gently for 3-4 minutes, stirring occasionally, until hot. Stir in chopped parsley and shelled clams.

Meanwhile, cook pasta in a large saucepan of lightly salted boiling water for 3 minutes, or until just cooked or al dente. Drain thoroughly, then serve on warmed plates. Spoon clam sauce over pasta and serve garnished with clams in their shells, and parsley sprigs if you like. Serve with a mixed green salad.

*Serves 4*

# — STILTON & WALNUT SAUCE —

350g (12oz) dried farfalle or spirali
salt and freshly ground black pepper
1 tablespoon olive oil
4 shallots, finely chopped
1 clove garlic, crushed
200g (7oz) crème fraîche
2 tablespoons chopped fresh chives
115g (4oz) walnut pieces
115g (4oz) Stilton cheese, crumbled
herb sprigs, to garnish

Cook pasta in a large saucepan of lightly salted boiling water for 10 minutes, or until just cooked or al dente.

Meanwhile, heat oil in a saucepan, add shallots and garlic and cook gently for 8-10 minutes, stirring occasionally, until softened. Stir in crème fraîche and heat gently until bubbling. Stir in chopped chives and salt and pepper.

Drain pasta thoroughly and return to rinsed-out pan. Add cream sauce, walnuts and Stilton and toss well to mix. Serve on warmed plates and garnish with herb sprigs. Serve with warm crusty bread rolls.

*Serves 4*

VARIATION: Use other blue cheese such as Gorgonzola, Dolcelatte or Cambozola (blue Brie) in place of Stilton.

# — CHUNKY TOMATO & BASIL —

1 tablespoon olive oil
6 shallots, finely chopped
2 cloves garlic, finely chopped
2 sticks celery, finely chopped
700g (1½lb) ripe plum tomatoes, skinned, seeded
   and roughly chopped
4 sun-dried tomatoes in oil, drained and chopped
150ml (5fl oz) red wine
1 tablespoon tomato purée
salt and freshly ground black pepper
350g (12oz) dried orecchiette
3-4 tablespoons chopped fresh basil

Heat oil in a large saucepan, add shallots, garlic and celery and cook gently for 5 minutes, stirring occasionally.

Add tomatoes, sun-dried tomatoes, wine, tomato purée and salt and pepper and mix well. Bring to the boil, then reduce heat, cover and simmer for 10 minutes, stirring occasionally. Uncover pan, increase heat slightly and cook for a further 10-15 minutes, stirring frequently, until sauce has thickened slightly.

Meanwhile, cook pasta in a large saucepan of lightly salted boiling water for 12-15 minutes, or until just cooked or al dente. Drain thoroughly and return to rinsed-out pan. Add tomato sauce and chopped basil and toss well to mix. Serve on warmed plates, and garnish with basil sprigs if you like. Serve with hot cheese-topped garlic bread.

*Serves 4*

# - GARLIC & CHILLI TAGLIATELLE -

350g (12oz) dried tricolour tagliatelle
salt and freshly ground black pepper
4 tablespoons olive oil
2 shallots, finely chopped
2 small fresh red chillies, seeded and finely chopped
3 cloves garlic, crushed
4 sun-dried tomatoes in oil, drained and chopped
3 tablespoons chopped fresh basil
85g (3oz) fresh Parmesan cheese, finely grated,
  to serve
basil sprigs, to garnish

Cook pasta in a large saucepan of lightly salted boiling water for 10-12 minutes, or until just cooked or al dente.

Meanwhile, heat 1 tablespoon oil in a large saucepan, add shallots, chillies and garlic and cook over a moderate heat for about 5 minutes, stirring frequently, until softened. Add remaining oil to pan with sun-dried tomatoes and salt and pepper and heat gently until hot.

Drain pasta thoroughly and return to rinsed-out pan. Add oil mixture with chopped basil and toss well to mix. Serve on warmed plates and sprinkle generously with Parmesan cheese. Garnish with basil sprigs and serve with crusty French bread.

*Serves 4*

VARIATION: Use fresh green chillies in place of red chillies.

## —— ROAST PEPPER & FENNEL ——

4 fennel bulbs
4 red peppers, seeded and cut into thick slices
5 tablespoons olive oil
juice of 1 lemon
salt and freshly ground black pepper
500g (1lb 2oz) fresh strozzapretti
225g (8oz) mozzarella cheese, diced
2 tablespoons chopped fresh flat-leaf parsley
flat-leaf parsley sprigs, to garnish

Preheat oven to 200C (400F/Gas 6). Trim fennel bulbs, cutting off fibrous tops. Cut each bulb into quarters and remove and discard core.

Cook fennel in a saucepan of boiling water for 5 minutes. Drain thoroughly. Lightly grease a shallow ovenproof dish or baking tin. Put fennel in the prepared dish with peppers. Whisk oil, lemon juice and salt and pepper together and drizzle over fennel and peppers. Toss gently to mix. Bake in the oven for about 30 minutes, stirring once or twice, until vegetables are tender and tinged brown around edges. Meanwhile, cook pasta in a large saucepan of lightly salted boiling water for 3 minutes, or until just cooked or al dente.

Scatter mozzarella and chopped parsley over vegetables and stir gently to mix. Drain pasta thoroughly and serve on warmed plates. Spoon vegetable mixture and juices over pasta. Alternatively, lightly toss the vegetables, cheese and pasta together before serving. Garnish with parsley sprigs and serve with warm crusty ciabatta bread.

*Serves 4*

VARIATION: Use yellow peppers in place of red peppers.

# HAZELNUT PESTO SAUCE

50g (2oz) basil leaves
50g (2oz) hazelnuts, lightly toasted
100ml (3½fl oz) olive oil
2 cloves garlic, crushed
85g (3oz) fresh Parmesan cheese, finely grated
salt and freshly ground black pepper
350g (12oz) dried plain or tomato spaghetti
basil sprigs, to garnish

Put basil leaves, hazelnuts, olive oil and garlic in a small blender or food processor and blend until smooth and well mixed.

Add Parmesan cheese and salt and pepper and blend briefly to mix. Transfer to a small bowl, cover and set aside. Cook pasta in a large saucepan of lightly salted boiling water for 10-12 minutes, or until just cooked or al dente. Drain thoroughly and return to rinsed-out pan.

Add pesto sauce and toss lightly to mix. Serve on warmed plates and garnish with basil sprigs. Serve with a mixed leaf salad.

*Serves 4*

VARIATIONS: Use lightly toasted pine nuts or almonds in place of hazelnuts. Use 25g (1oz) fresh parsley in place of 25g (1oz) basil.

# PARMESAN & PINE NUTS

350g (12oz) dried fusilli lunghi (long fusilli pasta)
salt and freshly ground black pepper
115g (4oz) pine nuts
50g (2oz) butter
1 small onion, finely chopped
2 courgettes, cut into thin strips
6 tablespoons crème fraîche
115g (4oz) fresh Parmesan cheese, finely grated
3 tablespoons chopped fresh flat-leaf parsley
herb sprigs, to garnish

Cook pasta in a large saucepan of lightly salted boiling water for 10-12 minutes, or until just cooked or al dente.

Meanwhile, preheat grill to high. Spread pine nuts out on a baking sheet and place under grill for 2-3 minutes, stirring occasionally, until lightly toasted all over. Remove from grill and set aside. Melt butter in a large frying pan, add onion and courgettes and cook for about 8 minutes, stirring occasionally, until tender. Stir in crème fraiche and pine nuts and heat gently until bubbling. Remove pan from heat, stir in half the Parmesan, the salt and pepper and mix well.

Drain pasta thoroughly and return to rinsed-out saucepan. Add pine nut sauce and chopped parsley and toss well to mix. Serve on warmed plates and sprinkle with remaining Parmesan. Garnish with herb sprigs and serve with warm crusty bread.

*Serves 4*

VARIATION: Use chopped fresh basil or coriander in place of parsley.

# – ASPARAGUS & GOAT'S CHEESE –

400g (14oz) extra fine asparagus, cut in half
50g (2oz) butter, melted
2 cloves garlic, crushed
150ml (5fl oz) double cream
3 tablespoons chopped fresh basil
salt and freshly ground black pepper
500g (1lb 2oz) fresh tagliatelle
175g (6oz) soft goat's cheese, crumbled
basil sprigs, to garnish

Steam asparagus over a pan of boiling water for 6-8 minutes or until just tender. Drain well.

Melt butter in a saucepan, add garlic and asparagus and cook for 1-2 minutes, stirring occasionally. Stir in cream, chopped basil and salt and pepper and heat gently until hot, stirring occasionally. Meanwhile, cook pasta in a large saucepan of lightly salted boiling water for 3 minutes, or until just cooked or al dente. Drain thoroughly and return to rinsed-out saucepan.

Add asparagus sauce and goat's cheese to pasta and toss lightly to mix. Serve on warmed plates and garnish with basil sprigs. Serve with a mixed baby leaf salad.

*Serves 4*

VARIATION: Use other cheese such as Brie or feta in place of goat's cheese.

## CLASSIC LASAGNE

1 tablespoon olive oil
2 onions, chopped
1 clove garlic, crushed
2 carrots, finely chopped
500g (1lb 2oz) lean minced beef
175g (6oz) mushrooms, chopped
400g (14oz) can chopped tomatoes
2 tablespoons tomato purée
200ml (7fl oz) dry white wine
2 teaspoons dried Italian herb seasoning
salt and freshly ground black pepper
70g (2½oz) butter
70g (2½oz) plain flour
850ml (30fl oz) milk
225g (8oz) Cheddar or pecorino cheese, grated
9 fresh lasagne sheets

Heat oil in a large pan, add onions, garlic and carrots and cook for 5 minutes, stirring. Add beef and cook until browned. Stir in mushrooms, tomatoes, tomato purée, wine, herbs and salt and pepper, and mix well. Bring to the boil, reduce heat, cover and simmer for 45 minutes, stirring occasionally. Preheat oven to 180C (350F/Gas 4). Lightly grease a large ovenproof dish; set aside. Melt butter in a saucepan, add flour and cook gently for 1 minute, stirring. Gradually whisk in milk, then heat gently, whisking continuously, until thick and smooth. Simmer for 2 minutes.

Remove pan from heat, whisk in 150g (5oz) cheese, then cover sauce with greaseproof paper; set aside. Part-cook lasagne according to packet directions. Remove from pan, refresh under cold running water, and drain on paper towels. Spoon one-third of meat sauce into prepared dish, cover with 3 sheets of lasagne and top with some cheese sauce. Repeat twice, pouring remaining cheese sauce over pasta. Sprinkle with remaining cheese. Bake for 45 minutes or until golden.

*Serves 4-6*

# BEEF & MACARONI PIE

1 tablespoon sunflower oil
1 onion, chopped
1 clove garlic, crushed
1 stick celery, finely chopped
2 small fresh red chillies, seeded and finely chopped
350g (12oz) lean minced beef
115g (4oz) button mushrooms, chopped
1 red pepper, seeded and diced
400g (14oz) can chopped tomatoes
150ml (5fl oz) dry white wine
salt and freshly ground black pepper
225g (8oz) dried short-cut macaroni
350g (12oz) Greek yogurt
2 eggs
50g (2oz) fresh Parmesan cheese, finely grated
herb sprigs, to garnish

Heat oil in a large saucepan, add onion, garlic, celery and chillies and cook for 5 minutes, stirring occasionally. Add beef and cook until browned all over, stirring. Add mushrooms, red pepper, tomatoes, wine and salt and pepper, and mix well. Bring to the boil, then reduce heat, cover and simmer for 45 minutes, stirring occasionally. Preheat oven to 190C (375F/Gas 5). Lightly grease an ovenproof dish and set aside. Cook macaroni in a large saucepan of lightly salted boiling water for 8-10 minutes, or until just cooked. Drain thoroughly.

Mix meat sauce and macaroni together and spoon into prepared dish. Lightly whisk yogurt, eggs and salt and pepper together and pour evenly over macaroni mixture. Sprinkle Parmesan over the top. Bake in the oven for 30 minutes, or until golden brown. Garnish with herb sprigs and serve with a mixed dark leaf salad.

*Serves 4-6*

VARIATION: Use lean minced lamb or pork in place of beef.

# LAMB & PEPPER BAKE

1 tablespoon olive oil
2 shallots, finely chopped
1 leek, washed and finely chopped
2 cloves garlic, crushed
1 small green pepper, seeded and finely chopped
350g (12oz) lean minced lamb
200ml (7fl oz) passata
1 tablespoon chopped fresh oregano
1 tablespoon chopped fresh thyme
salt and freshly ground black pepper
12 fresh lasagne sheets
400g (14oz) natural whole milk yogurt
2 eggs
85g (3oz) Gruyère cheese, finely grated
herb sprigs, to garnish

Heat oil in a saucepan, add shallots, leek, garlic and green pepper and cook for 5 minutes, stirring occasionally. Add lamb and cook until browned all over, stirring frequently. Stir in passata, chopped herbs and salt and pepper, and mix well. Bring to the boil, then reduce heat, cover and simmer for 20 minutes, stirring occasionally. Uncover, increase the heat slightly and cook for a further 8-10 minutes, stirring frequently, until most of liquid has evaporated. Preheat the oven to 200C (400F/Gas 6). Lightly butter a shallow ovenproof dish and set aside.

Cook lasagne in a large pan of lightly salted boiling water for 2 minutes, drain, refresh under cold running water; drain again. Lay lasagne out on work surface and spoon some lamb mixture along long edge of each sheet. Roll lasagne to make cannelloni. Arrange cannelloni, seam-side down, in prepared dish. Lightly beat yogurt, eggs and salt and pepper together and pour over cannelloni. Sprinkle cheese over top. Bake for 25-30 minutes, or until golden. Garnish with herb sprigs.

*Serves 4-6*

# —— TAGLIATELLE CARBONARA ——

350g (12oz) dried tagliatelle
salt and freshly ground black pepper
25g (1oz) butter
1 tablespoon olive oil
1 onion, finely chopped
225g (8oz) smoked back bacon rashers, chopped
3 eggs, beaten
6 tablespoons double cream
50g (2oz) pecorino cheese, finely grated
85g (3oz) fresh Parmesan cheese, finely grated
chopped fresh chives, to garnish

Cook pasta in a large saucepan of lightly salted boiling water for 10-12 minutes, or until just cooked or al dente.

Meanwhile, heat butter and oil in a saucepan until butter is melted. Add onion and cook for 5 minutes, stirring occasionally, until softened. Add bacon and cook for 5 minutes, stirring frequently, until bacon is cooked. Remove pan from the heat and set aside. Mix eggs, cream, pecorino cheese, 50g (2oz) Parmesan and salt and pepper together in a bowl. Drain pasta thoroughly and return to a clean pan. Add bacon mixture and toss to mix.

Add egg mixture and cook gently, tossing continuously until eggs are just cooked. Serve, sprinkled with remaining Parmesan. Garnish with chopped fresh chives and serve with fresh crusty bread.

*Serves 4*

VARIATIONS: Use Cheddar cheese in place of pecorino. Use spaghetti or bucatini in place of tagliatelle.

# — FENNEL & BACON GRATIN —

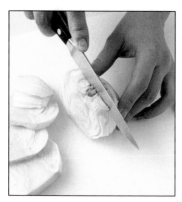

3 fennel bulbs, trimmed
salt and freshly ground black pepper
50g (2oz) butter
225g (8oz) dried penne
225g (8oz) rindless smoked back bacon rashers, chopped
4 tablespoons plain flour
450ml (16fl oz) milk
150ml (5fl oz) double cream
115g (4oz) Cheddar cheese, grated
3 tablespoons fresh breadcrumbs
herb sprigs, to garnish

Cut fennel lengthways into 5mm (¼in) slices. Cook in a pan of lightly salted boiling water for 10-15 minutes or until tender.

Remove from pan using a slotted spoon. Set pan and cooking water aside. Put fennel in a bowl, add 15g (½oz) butter and toss to mix. Set aside and keep warm. Cook pasta in reserved pan of boiling cooking water for 10 minutes, or until just cooked or al dente. Melt 15g (½oz) of remaining butter in a pan, add bacon and cook over a fairly high heat for 5 minutes, stirring, until bacon is cooked. Remove bacon from pan using a slotted spoon and add to fennel. Set aside and keep hot. Add remaining butter to juices in pan; heat, add flour and cook for 1 minute, stirring.

Gradually whisk in milk and cream, heat gently, whisking, until sauce is thickened. Simmer for 2 minutes, stirring. Remove pan from heat and whisk in 85g (3oz) cheese and salt and pepper. Drain pasta thoroughly and toss with fennel and bacon. Pour cheese sauce over pasta and toss to mix. Transfer to a flameproof dish. Preheat grill to high. Mix remaining cheese and breadcrumbs and sprinkle over the top. Grill for a few minutes until golden. Garnish with herb sprigs.

*Serves 4*

# — PEA, HAM & PARSLEY BAKE —

225g (8oz) dried rigatoni
salt and freshly ground black pepper
40g (1½oz) butter
40g (1½oz) plain flour
850ml (30fl oz) milk
225g (8oz) lean smoked ham, diced
225g (8oz) frozen peas
4 tablespoons chopped fresh parsley
50g (2oz) Cheddar cheese, grated (optional)
flat-leaf parsley sprigs, to garnish

Preheat the oven to 200C (400F/Gas 6). Lightly butter an ovenproof dish; set aside.

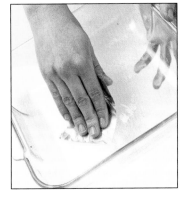

Cook pasta in a large saucepan of lightly salted boiling water for about 10 minutes, or until just cooked or al dente. Drain well, set aside and keep warm. Meanwhile, put butter, flour and milk in a separate saucepan. Heat gently, whisking continuously, until sauce is thickened and smooth. Simmer gently for 3 minutes, stirring. Remove pan from the heat, add pasta, ham, peas, chopped parsley and salt and pepper and stir gently to mix.

Transfer to prepared dish and sprinkle with Cheddar cheese, if using. Bake in the oven for 20-25 minutes, or until lightly browned and bubbling. Garnish with parsley sprigs and serve with cooked vegetables such as green beans and grilled tomatoes.

*Serves 4*

VARIATIONS: Use cooked smoked chicken or turkey in place of ham. Use fresh Parmesan cheese in place of Cheddar.

# — PANCETTA & CHILLI PENNE —

700g (1½lb) plum tomatoes
40g (1½oz) butter
6 shallots, finely chopped
1 large clove garlic, crushed
2 fresh red chillies, seeded and finely chopped
2 sticks celery, finely chopped
225g (8oz) pancetta, diced
175g (6oz) mushrooms, finely chopped
150ml (5fl oz) red wine
4 sun-dried tomatoes in oil, drained and chopped
salt and freshly ground black pepper
500g (1lb 2oz) fresh penne rigate
2 tablespoons chopped fresh oregano
oregano sprigs, to garnish

Put plum tomatoes in a large bowl and cover with boiling water. Leave for 30-60 seconds, then drain and peel; deseed them and chop the flesh. Set aside. Melt butter in a saucepan, add shallots, garlic, chillies, celery and pancetta and cook for 5 minutes, stirring. Add chopped plum tomatoes, mushrooms, wine, sun-dried tomatoes and salt and pepper, and stir to mix. Bring to the boil, then cover and simmer for 10 minutes, stirring occasionally. Uncover pan, increase heat slightly and cook for 10-15 minutes, stirring occasionally, until sauce has thickened slightly.

Meanwhile, cook pasta in a large saucepan of lightly salted boiling water for 3-5 minutes, or until just cooked or al dente. Drain thoroughly and return to the rinsed-out pan. Add tomato sauce and chopped oregano and toss well to mix. Garnish with oregano sprigs and serve with a mixed leaf salad and hot crusty garlic bread.

*Serves 4*

VARIATION: Use chorizo in place of pancetta.

# — SPICED PORK SPAGHETTINI —

1 tablespoon sunflower oil
2 red onions, chopped
1 large red pepper, seeded and diced
350g (12oz) lean minced pork
1 tablespoon plain flour
2 teaspoons ground cumin
1½ teaspoons hot chilli powder
1 teaspoon ground coriander
400g (14oz) can chopped tomatoes
2 tablespoons tomato purée
300ml (10fl oz) pork or vegetable stock
salt and freshly ground black pepper
225g (8oz) chestnut mushrooms, sliced
500g (1lb 2oz) fresh spaghettini
herb sprigs, to garnish

Heat oil in a large saucepan, add onions and red pepper and cook gently for 5 minutes, stirring occasionally. Add minced pork and cook until browned all over, stirring frequently. Add flour and ground spices and cook for 1 minute, stirring. Stir in tomatoes, tomato purée, stock and salt and pepper, and mix well. Bring to the boil, then reduce the heat, cover and simmer for 30 minutes, stirring occasionally.

Stir in mushrooms, cover and simmer for a further 30 minutes, stirring occasionally. Meanwhile, cook pasta in a large pan of lightly salted boiling water for 3 minutes, or until just cooked or al dente. Drain thoroughly and serve on warmed plates. Spoon sauce over pasta and garnish with herb sprigs. Serve with warm crusty bread.

*Serves 4-6*

VARIATION: Use lean minced lamb or turkey in place of pork.

# TORTELLONI GRATIN

225g (8oz) small broccoli florets
450g (1lb) fresh ham and cheese tortelloni
salt and freshly ground black pepper
85g (3oz) butter
4 shallots, finely chopped
115g (4oz) button mushrooms, sliced
50g (2oz) plain flour
550ml (20fl oz) milk
150ml (5fl oz) double cream
115g (4oz) pecorino cheese, grated
3 tablespoons fresh breadcrumbs
herb sprigs, to garnish

Cook broccoli in a large saucepan of boiling water for 5 minutes, or until tender. Drain well, set aside and keep warm.

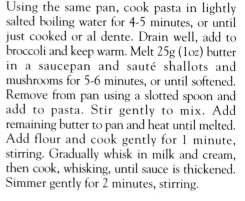

Using the same pan, cook pasta in lightly salted boiling water for 4-5 minutes, or until just cooked or al dente. Drain well, add to broccoli and keep warm. Melt 25g (1oz) butter in a saucepan and sauté shallots and mushrooms for 5-6 minutes, or until softened. Remove from pan using a slotted spoon and add to pasta. Stir gently to mix. Add remaining butter to pan and heat until melted. Add flour and cook gently for 1 minute, stirring. Gradually whisk in milk and cream, then cook, whisking, until sauce is thickened. Simmer gently for 2 minutes, stirring.

Remove pan from the heat and whisk in 85g (3oz) pecorino cheese. Pour cheese sauce over pasta and vegetables and toss well to mix. Preheat grill to high. Transfer pasta mixture to a flameproof dish. Mix together remaining cheese and breadcrumbs and sprinkle over the top. Place under grill for 2-3 minutes or until golden and bubbling. Garnish with herb sprigs and serve with cooked vegetables such as baby carrots and courgettes.

*Serves 4-6*

# TOMATO & CHORIZO TORTELLINI

2 tablespoons olive oil
1 red onion, finely chopped
1 red pepper, seeded and diced
2 carrots, finely chopped
2 cloves garlic, crushed
175g (6oz) chorizo, thinly sliced
400g (14oz) can chopped tomatoes
4 tablespoons dry white wine
2 tablespoons sun-dried tomato paste
salt and freshly ground black pepper
400g (14oz) dried tortellini, such as cheese
   and ham tortellini
3 tablespoons chopped fresh basil
fresh Parmesan cheese shavings, to garnish

Heat oil in a saucepan, add onion, red pepper, carrots and garlic and cook for 5 minutes, stirring occasionally. Add chorizo and cook for 1 minute, stirring. Add tomatoes, wine, tomato paste and salt and pepper and mix well. Bring to the boil, then reduce heat, cover and simmer for 15 minutes, stirring occasionally. Uncover, increase heat slightly and cook for a further 10-15 minutes, stirring occasionally, until sauce is cooked and has thickened slightly.

Meanwhile, cook pasta in a large saucepan of lightly salted boiling water for 10 minutes, or until cooked and tender. Drain pasta thoroughly and return it to the rinsed-out pan. Add chorizo sauce and chopped basil and toss well to mix. Serve on warmed plates and garnish with shavings of Parmesan cheese. Serve with hot crusty garlic and herb bread.

*Serves 4*

# -TURKEY & BROCCOLI LASAGNE-

300g (10oz) small broccoli florets
1 tablespoon sunflower oil
1 onion, chopped
1 clove garlic, crushed
2 sticks celery, finely chopped
225g (8oz) mushrooms, sliced
2 courgettes, sliced
40g (1½oz) butter
40g (1½oz) plain flour
850ml (30fl oz) milk
175g (6oz) Cheddar cheese, grated
salt and freshly ground black pepper
400g (14oz) cooked skinless, boneless turkey
  breast, diced
8 sheets no pre-cook lasagne verdi
herb sprigs, to garnish

Preheat the oven to 180C (350F/Gas 4).
Lightly grease a shallow ovenproof dish and
set aside. Cook broccoli in a saucepan of
boiling water for 2 minutes. Drain well and
set aside. Heat oil in a large saucepan, add
onion, garlic, celery, mushrooms and
courgettes and cook for 5 minutes, stirring
occasionally. Meanwhile, melt butter in a
separate saucepan, add flour and cook gently
for 1 minute, stirring. Gradually whisk in
milk, then heat gently, whisking, until the
sauce is thickened and smooth. Simmer
gently for 2 minutes, stirring.

Remove pan from heat and stir in 150g (5oz)
cheese and salt and pepper. Set aside 300ml
(10fl oz) cheese sauce. Mix remaining sauce
with vegetables, broccoli and turkey. Spoon
half turkey mixture into prepared dish and
cover with half the lasagne. Repeat these
layers, then pour reserved cheese sauce over
lasagne, to cover. Sprinkle with remaining
cheese. Bake for 45 minutes, or until cooked
and golden. Garnish with herb sprigs and
serve with a mixed green salad.

Serves 4-6

# — CAJUN CHICKEN FETTUCCINE —

1 tablespoon sunflower oil
6 shallots, thinly sliced
1 green pepper, seeded and sliced
2 carrots, cut into matchstick strips
225g (8oz) button mushrooms, halved
450g (1lb) skinless, boneless chicken breast,
  cut into thin strips
1 tablespoon Cajun seasoning
1 tablespoon cornflour
2 tablespoons dry sherry
300ml (10fl oz) chicken stock
2 tablespoons tomato purée
salt and freshly ground black pepper
500g (1lb 2oz) fresh fettuccine
chopped fresh parsley, to garnish

Heat oil in a wok or large frying pan, add shallots, green pepper, carrots and mushrooms and stir-fry for 3 minutes. Add chicken and stir-fry for a further 3-4 minutes, or until cooked, then add Cajun seasoning and stir-fry for 1 minute. Blend cornflour with sherry and add to the wok with stock, tomato purée and salt and pepper. Stir-fry until hot and bubbling, then simmer gently for 2-3 minutes.

Meanwhile, cook pasta in a large saucepan of lightly salted boiling water for 3 minutes, or until just cooked or al dente. Drain thoroughly and serve on warmed plates. Spoon chicken sauce over pasta and sprinkle with chopped parsley to garnish. Serve with warm crusty bread.

*Serves 4*

VARIATIONS: Use turkey breast or lean pork or beef in place of chicken. Use Chinese 5-spice seasoning in place of Cajun seasoning.

# CHICKEN CANNELLONI

225g (8oz) cooked skinless, boneless chicken
 breast, finely chopped
115g (4oz) full fat soft cheese
50g (2oz) pine nuts, toasted and finely chopped
50g (2oz) sultanas
4 spring onions, finely chopped
2 eggs, beaten
2 tablespoons chopped fresh coriander
salt and freshly ground black pepper
16 dried cannelloni tubes
40g (1½oz) butter
40g (1½oz) plain flour
550ml (20fl oz) milk
50g (2oz) fresh Parmesan cheese, finely grated
coriander sprigs, to garnish

Preheat the oven to 180C (350F/Gas 4).
Lightly grease a shallow ovenproof dish and
set aside. Put chicken, soft cheese, pine
nuts, sultanas, spring onions, eggs, chopped
coriander and salt and pepper in a bowl and
mix well. Set aside. Part-cook cannelloni
tubes according to packet directions.
Remove from pan, refresh under cold
running water, then drain well on paper
towels. Fill each cannelloni tube with
chicken mixture. Arrange filled tubes in a
single layer in prepared dish. Set aside.

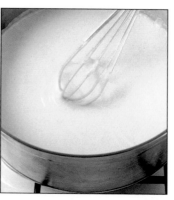

Put butter, flour and milk in a saucepan and
heat gently, whisking continuously, until
sauce is thickened and smooth. Simmer for
3 minutes, stirring. Pour sauce over filled
cannelloni tubes and sprinkle cheese over
the top. Bake for 35-40 minutes, or until
golden brown. Garnish with coriander sprigs
and serve with a mixed green salad.

*Serves 4*

VARIATION: Use cooked smoked or
unsmoked turkey breast in place of chicken.

# - SMOKED CHICKEN & LEEK BAKE -

225g (8oz) dried tricolour trompretti or fusilli
salt and freshly ground black pepper
85g (3oz) butter
3 leeks, washed and sliced
225g (8oz) mushrooms, sliced
1 yellow pepper, seeded and sliced
50g (2oz) plain flour
450ml (16fl oz) chicken stock
450ml (16fl oz) milk
150g (5oz) Cheddar cheese, grated
225g (8oz) cooked skinless, boneless smoked
    chicken, diced
3 tablespoons chopped fresh parsley
parsley sprigs, to garnish

Preheat oven to 200C (400F/Gas 6). Lightly
grease an ovenproof dish and set aside. Cook
pasta in a large saucepan of lightly salted
boiling water for 10 minutes, or until just
cooked or al dente. Meanwhile, melt 25g
(1oz) butter in a frying pan, add leeks,
mushrooms and yellow pepper and cook over
a fairly high heat for 5 minutes, stirring
occasionally, until softened. Remove pan
from heat and set aside. Put remaining butter,
flour, stock and milk in a saucepan and heat
gently, whisking, until sauce is thickened.
Simmer gently for 3 minutes, stirring.

Remove pan from heat and stir in 115g
(4oz) cheese, the chicken, chopped parsley
and salt and pepper. Drain pasta thoroughly
and add to chicken sauce with leeks,
mushrooms and yellow pepper and mix well.
Transfer to prepared dish and sprinkle with
remaining cheese. Bake for 25-30 minutes,
or until golden brown and bubbling.
Garnish with parsley sprigs and serve with
crusty bread and a mixed baby leaf salad.

*Serves 4*

# - CHICKEN & COURGETTE PASTA -

50g (2oz) butter
6 shallots, thinly sliced
3 courgettes, cut into matchstick strips
100ml (3½fl oz) dry white wine
350g (12oz) dried fusilli lunghi (long fusilli pasta)
salt and freshly ground black pepper
350g (12oz) cooked skinless, boneless chicken
  breast, cut into thin strips
1 tablespoon chopped fresh tarragon
300g (10oz) crème fraîche
85g (3oz) fresh Parmesan cheese, finely grated
tarragon sprigs, to garnish

Melt butter in a saucepan, add shallots and courgettes and cook gently for 10 minutes, stirring occasionally, until softened.

Add wine and cook over a moderate heat until reduced by half. Meanwhile, cook pasta in a large pan of lightly salted boiling water for 10-12 minutes, or until just cooked or al dente. Add chicken, chopped tarragon and salt and pepper to shallot mixture, reduce heat and cook for 2 minutes, stirring.

Stir in crème fraîche and heat gently until hot and bubbling. Stir in Parmesan. Drain pasta thoroughly and return to the rinsed-out pan. Add chicken sauce and toss well to mix. Serve on warmed plates and garnish with tarragon sprigs. Serve with additional Parmesan and warm crusty bread.

*Serves 4*

VARIATIONS: Use cooked turkey breast or cooked flaked salmon in place of chicken. Use 1 large onion in place of shallots.

# — GRILLED SCALLOP CAPELLINI —

40g (1½oz) basil leaves
15g (½oz) fresh flat-leaf parsley
25g (1oz) pine nuts
2 cloves garlic, crushed
50g (2oz) sun-dried tomatoes in oil
  (drained weight)
1 tablespoon tomato purée
8 tablespoons olive oil
50g (2oz) fresh Parmesan cheese, finely grated
salt and freshly ground black pepper
450g (1lb) shelled medium scallops
500g (1lb 2oz) fresh capellini
basil sprigs, to garnish

Put first 6 ingredients in a small blender or food processor with 6 tablespoons oil and blend well. Add Parmesan and salt and pepper and blend briefly. Set aside. Preheat grill to high. Thread scallops on to wooden skewers (soak skewers in water before use to prevent scorching under grill). Brush with remaining oil and season with salt and plenty of black pepper. Grill for 10 minutes, or until cooked and just firm, turning once. Remove scallops from skewers and cut them in half or quarters. Set aside and keep hot.

Meanwhile, cook pasta in a large saucepan of lightly salted boiling water for 3 minutes, or until just cooked or al dente. In the meantime, gently heat the pesto (basil sauce) in a saucepan until hot, stirring occasionally. Drain pasta thoroughly, then return to the rinsed-out pan. Add pesto and toss well to mix, then add scallops and toss gently. Serve on warmed plates and garnish with basil sprigs. Serve with crusty French bread.

*Serves 4*

# — SMOKED HADDOCK LASAGNE —

500g (1lb 2oz) skinless smoked haddock fillet
2 bay leaves
850ml (30fl oz) milk
1 tablespoon sunflower oil
1 onion, chopped
2 sticks celery, finely chopped
2 courgettes, sliced
175g (6oz) mushrooms, sliced
40g (1½oz) butter
40g (1½oz) plain flour
175g (6oz) Cheddar cheese, grated
9 fresh lasagne sheets
225g (8oz) frozen peas
3 tablespoons chopped fresh parsley
salt and freshly ground black pepper
3 tablespoons fresh breadcrumbs

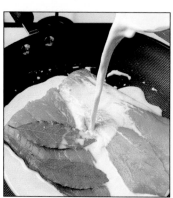

Preheat oven to 190C (375F/Gas 5). Put fish in a pan with bay leaves and milk. Cover, bring to the boil, then simmer for 6-8 minutes. Heat oil in a saucepan, add onion and celery and cook for 5 minutes, stirring. Add courgettes and mushrooms and cook for 5 minutes; set aside. Remove fish from milk using a slotted spoon; flake flesh. Discard bay leaves; reserve milk. Melt butter in a saucepan, stir in flour and cook gently for 1 minute. Whisk in reserved milk, then cook, whisking, until thickened. Simmer for 2 minutes. Whisk in 150g (5oz) cheese; cover and set aside.

Part-cook lasagne according to packet directions. Refresh under cold running water, then drain on paper towels. Drain off liquid from onion mixture. Reserve 300ml (10fl oz) cheese sauce and mix remaining sauce with fish, cooked vegetables, peas, parsley and salt and pepper. Spoon one-third of fish sauce into ovenproof dish; cover with 3 lasagne sheets. Repeat twice more; pour reserved cheese sauce over. Mix remaining cheese with breadcrumbs; sprinkle over top. Bake for 30-40 minutes.

*Serves 4*

# —CREAMY SALMON FETTUCCINE—

25g (1oz) butter
225g (8oz) button mushrooms, halved
150ml (5fl oz) dry white wine
300g (10oz) crème fraîche
300g (10oz) smoked salmon, cut into thin strips
　or small chunks
1 tablespoon chopped fresh dill
1 tablespoon creamed horseradish
salt and freshly ground black pepper
500g (1lb 2oz) fresh fettuccine
dill sprigs, to garnish

Melt butter in a saucepan, add mushrooms and cook over a moderate heat for 5 minutes, stirring occasionally.

Add wine, bring to the boil and cook over a high heat until reduced by half. Reduce the heat, stir in crème fraîche and bring gently to the boil. Stir in salmon, chopped dill, horseradish and salt and pepper and heat gently for a minute or two. Meanwhile, cook pasta in a large saucepan of lightly salted boiling water for 3 minutes, or until just cooked or al dente.

Drain pasta thoroughly and return to the rinsed-out pan. Add salmon sauce and toss well to mix. Serve on warmed plates and garnish with dill sprigs. Serve with cooked fresh vegetables such as broccoli florets and baby carrots.

*Serves 4*

VARIATIONS: Use sliced courgettes in place of mushrooms. Use double cream in place of crème fraîche.

# —— PESTO COD CANNELLONI ——

350g (12oz) skinless cod fillet
2 bay leaves
2 shallots, cut into quarters
300ml (10fl oz) milk
25g (1oz) butter
85g (3oz) mushrooms, finely chopped
1 small courgette, finely chopped
4 tablespoons pesto
salt and freshly ground black pepper
12 cannelloni tubes
15g (½oz) plain flour
115g (4oz) Cheddar or pecorino cheese, grated
3 tablespoons fresh breadcrumbs
basil sprigs, to garnish

Preheat oven to 190C (375F/Gas 5). Put fish in a saucepan with bay leaves, shallots and milk. Cover, bring gently to the boil, then simmer for 6-8 minutes or until fish flakes. Meanwhile, melt 15g (½oz) butter in a saucepan, add mushrooms and courgette and sauté for 5 minutes. Remove pan from heat. Remove fish from milk using a slotted spoon and flake flesh. Remove and discard bay leaves and shallots and reserve milk. Add fish to mushroom mixture, together with pesto and salt and pepper; mix well. Set aside. Part-cook cannelloni according to packet directions.

Refresh cannelloni under cold running water; drain well. Fill with fish mixture and arrange in a single layer in a shallow ovenproof dish. Set aside. Put milk in a saucepan with remaining butter and flour. Heat gently, whisking, until sauce is thickened. Simmer for 3 minutes, stirring. Remove from heat; stir in 85g (3oz) cheese. Pour sauce over cannelloni. Mix remaining cheese and breadcrumbs and sprinkle over top. Bake for 30-40 minutes, or until golden. Garnish with basil sprigs.

*Serves 4*

# ——— TAGLIATELLE NIÇOISE ———

350g (12oz) dried tagliatelle
salt and freshly ground black pepper
225g (8oz) green beans, halved
4 tablespoons olive oil
1 clove garlic, crushed
2 tablespoons red pesto
2 tablespoons apple juice
400g (14oz) can tuna in oil, drained and flaked
4 plum tomatoes, skinned and quartered
25g (1oz) pitted black olives, roughly chopped
50g (2oz) can anchovy fillets, drained and
    cut in half lengthways
1 tablespoon chopped fresh parsley
1 tablespoon chopped fresh basil
2 eggs, hard-boiled, shelled and quartered,
    to garnish (optional)

Cook pasta in a large saucepan of lightly salted boiling water for 10-12 minutes, or until just cooked or al dente. Meanwhile, cook green beans in a separate saucepan of boiling water for 5-6 minutes, or until cooked and tender. Drain well, set aside and rinse out and dry the saucepan. Heat oil in the pan, add garlic and cook gently for 2 minutes. Whisk in pesto and apple juice and simmer gently for 1 minute. Drain pasta and return to the rinsed-out pan.

Add oil mixture and toss well to mix. Add green beans, tuna, tomatoes, olives, anchovies, chopped herbs and salt and pepper and toss to mix. Serve on warmed plates and garnish with egg quarters, if using. Serve with crusty French bread.

*Serves 4*

VARIATIONS: Use canned salmon in place of tuna. Use cooked broad beans or runner beans in place of green beans.

# — TASTY TUNA SPAGHETTINI —

50g (2oz) butter
225g (8oz) leeks, washed and sliced
225g (8oz) chestnut mushrooms, sliced
25g (1oz) plain flour
300ml (10fl oz) milk
150ml (5fl oz) double cream
400g (14oz) can tuna in oil, drained and flaked
50g (2oz) pitted black olives, chopped
3 tablespoons chopped fresh parsley
good pinch of cayenne pepper
salt and freshly ground black pepper
350g (12oz) dried spaghettini
marjoram sprigs, to garnish

Melt butter in a pan, add leeks and mushrooms and cook for 10 minutes, stirring occasionally, until soft. Add flour and cook gently for 1 minute, stirring. Remove pan from heat and gradually whisk in milk and cream, then cook, stirring continuously, until sauce is thickened and smooth. Simmer gently for 2 minutes, stirring. Stir in tuna, olives, chopped parsley, cayenne pepper and salt and pepper and reheat gently until piping hot, stirring.

Meanwhile, cook pasta in a large saucepan of lightly salted boiling water for 10-12 minutes, or until just cooked or al dente. Drain thoroughly and serve on warmed plates. Spoon tuna sauce over pasta and garnish with marjoram sprigs. Serve with fresh crusty bread and a mixed leaf salad.

*Serves 4*

VARIATION: Grill or bake about 300g (10oz) fresh tuna steaks until cooked, then flake and add to sauce in place of canned tuna.

# — SPICED MUSSEL LINGUINE —

1 tablespoon olive oil
1 red onion, finely chopped
1 red pepper, seeded and finely diced
2 cloves garlic, crushed
2 small fresh chillies, seeded and finely chopped
2 teaspoons ground coriander
2 teaspoons ground cumin
1 x 400g (14oz) can chopped tomatoes AND 1 x
    225g (8oz) can chopped tomatoes
150ml (5fl oz) dry white wine
2 tablespoons tomato purée
salt and freshly ground black pepper
350g (12oz) cooked, shelled mussels
500g (1lb 2oz) fresh linguine
8 cooked fresh mussels in their shells
herb sprigs, to garnish

Heat oil in a saucepan, add onion, red pepper, garlic and chillies and cook for 5 minutes, stirring. Add ground spices and cook for 1 minute, stirring. Stir in chopped tomatoes, wine, tomato purée and salt and pepper. Bring to the boil, then cook, uncovered, over a moderate heat for about 15 minutes, stirring occasionally, until sauce has thickened slightly. Stir in shelled mussels and cook for about 5 minutes, stirring occasionally, until piping hot.

Meanwhile, cook pasta in a large saucepan of lightly salted boiling water for 3 minutes, or until just cooked or al dente. Drain thoroughly and serve on warmed plates. Spoon mussel sauce over pasta and garnish with fresh mussels in their shells and herb sprigs. Alternatively, toss mussel sauce and cooked pasta together before serving. Serve with warm ciabatta bread and a mixed baby leaf salad.

*Serves 4*

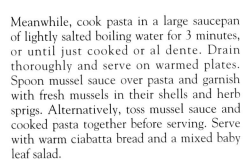

# STUFFED PASTA SHELLS

16 dried conchiglioni (large pasta shells)
salt and freshly ground black pepper
40g (1½oz) butter
3 shallots, finely chopped
1 red pepper, seeded and finely chopped
1 teaspoon grated fresh root ginger
2 x 170g (6oz) cans crab meat, drained
1 tablespoon chopped fresh coriander
225g (8oz) mushrooms, sliced
150ml (5fl oz) dry white wine
200ml (7fl oz) double cream
5 tablespoons finely grated fresh Parmesan cheese
coriander sprigs, to garnish

Preheat oven to 190C (375F/Gas 5). Cook pasta in a large saucepan of lightly salted boiling water for 10 minutes, or until just cooked or al dente. Meanwhile, melt 15g (½oz) butter in a pan, add shallots, red pepper and ginger and sauté for about 5 minutes, until soft. Remove pan from heat and stir in crab meat, chopped coriander and salt and pepper. Set aside. Drain pasta, rinse under cold running water and drain again. Set aside. Melt remaining butter in a saucepan, and cook mushrooms over a fairly high heat for about 5 minutes, stirring occasionally, until softened.

Add wine, bring to the boil and cook over a high heat until reduced by half. Stir in cream, 2 tablespoons Parmesan and salt and pepper and heat gently until bubbling. Remove pan from heat and keep hot. Fill pasta shells with crab mixture. Pour mushroom sauce into a shallow ovenproof dish and place filled pasta shells on top. Sprinkle remaining Parmesan over the top. Bake for 20 minutes, or until bubbling and golden. Garnish with coriander sprigs and serve with a mixed green salad.

*Serves 4*

# — TUNA & SWEETCORN BAKE —

1 tablespoon olive oil
1 onion, finely chopped
1 yellow pepper, seeded and diced
2 sticks celery, finely chopped
2 courgettes, finely diced
400g (14oz) can chopped tomatoes
150ml (5fl oz) dry white wine
2 teaspoons dried Italian herb seasoning
salt and freshly ground black pepper
300g (10oz) dried penne rigate
2 x 200g (7oz) cans sweetcorn kernels, drained
400g (14oz) can tuna in brine, drained and flaked
50g (2oz) fresh Parmesan cheese, finely grated
herb sprigs, to garnish

Preheat oven to 190C (375F/Gas 5). Heat oil in a saucepan, add onion, yellow pepper and celery and cook for 5 minutes, stirring occasionally. Stir in courgettes, tomatoes, wine, dried herbs and salt and pepper. Bring to the boil, then reduce heat, cover and simmer for 10 minutes, stirring occasionally. Uncover, increase heat slightly and cook for a further 5 minutes, or until sauce has reduced and thickened slightly. Meanwhile, cook pasta in a large saucepan of lightly salted boiling water for 10 minutes, or until just cooked or al dente. Drain and return to rinsed-out pan.

Add tomato sauce, sweetcorn and tuna and toss well to mix. Transfer to an ovenproof dish and sprinkle with Parmesan cheese. Bake for 20-25 minutes, or until bubbling and golden. Garnish with herb sprigs and serve with warm ciabatta bread.

*Serves 4-6*

VARIATIONS: Use canned salmon or cooked smoked cod or haddock in place of tuna. Use Cheddar or Gruyère cheese in place of Parmesan.

# — PEPPERED SALMON FUSILLI —

2 tablespoons mixed peppercorns
3 salmon steaks, each about 175g (6oz)
juice of 1 lime
350g (12oz) crème fraîche
4 spring onions, finely chopped
50g (2oz) watercress, chopped
salt and freshly ground black pepper
500g (1lb 2oz) fresh tricolore fusilli or conchiglie
dill sprigs, to garnish

Preheat grill to medium. Crush peppercorns coarsely using a pestle and mortar, then sprinkle on to a plate. Press each salmon steak into pepper, covering both sides completely.

Put salmon steaks on a rack in a grill pan and drizzle the lime juice over. Grill for 8-10 minutes, turning once, until flesh is cooked and is just beginning to flake. Skin and flake salmon, set aside and keep hot. Pour crème fraîche into a saucepan and heat gently until almost boiling. Add spring onions, watercress and salt and pepper and cook until heated through. Stir in salmon.

Meanwhile, cook pasta in a large saucepan of lightly salted boiling water for 3 minutes, or until just cooked or al dente. Drain pasta thoroughly and return to the rinsed-out pan. Add salmon sauce and toss well to mix. Serve on warmed plates and garnish with dill sprigs. Serve with fresh soft bread rolls and a mixed leaf salad.

*Serves 4*

VARIATION: Use tuna steaks in place of salmon.

# SPICED PRAWN STIR-FRY

1 tablespoon cornflour
100ml (3½fl oz) apple juice
2 tablespoons dry sherry
1 tablespoon light soy sauce
salt and freshly ground black pepper
350g (12oz) dried tomato or plain tagliatelle
1 tablespoon olive oil
6 shallots, thinly sliced
1 clove garlic, crushed
2.5cm (1in) piece fresh root ginger,
 peeled and finely chopped
1 tablespoon Chinese 5-spice seasoning
2 carrots, cut into thin matchstick strips
2 red peppers, seeded and sliced
175g (6oz) mange tout
350g (12oz) cooked shelled king or tiger prawns

In a small bowl, blend cornflour with apple juice, sherry, soy sauce and salt and pepper. Set aside. Cook pasta in a large saucepan of lightly salted boiling water for 10-12 minutes, or until just cooked or al dente. Meanwhile, heat oil in a wok or large frying pan, add shallots, garlic and ginger and stir-fry over a high heat for 1 minute.

Add Chinese 5-spice seasoning and stir-fry for 30 seconds, then add carrots and red peppers and stir-fry for 2-3 minutes. Add mange tout and prawns and stir-fry for a further 2-3 minutes. Add cornflour mixture, stir until mixture thickens, then stir-fry for a further 1-2 minutes. Drain pasta thoroughly and add to the wok. Toss to mix, then serve on warmed plates. Serve with a crisp mixed leaf salad.

*Serves 4*

# — SEAFOOD SOUFFLÉ LASAGNE —

70g (2½oz) butter
70g (2½oz) plain flour
1.2 litres (40fl oz) milk
300g (10oz) skinless salmon fillet or tuna steak, diced
225g (8oz) skinless cod or haddock fillet, diced
175g (6oz) cooked peeled prawns
225g (8oz) frozen peas
200g (7oz) can sweetcorn kernels, drained
2 tablespoons drained capers, roughly chopped
3 tablespoons chopped fresh parsley
1 tablespoon chopped fresh tarragon
salt and freshly ground black pepper
2 eggs, separated
9 no pre-cook lasagne sheets
4 tablespoons finely grated fresh Parmesan cheese
herb sprigs, to garnish

Preheat oven to 180C (350F/Gas 4). Put 50g (2oz) butter in a saucepan with 50g (2oz) flour and 850ml (30fl oz) milk. Heat gently, whisking, until sauce is thickened and smooth. Simmer gently for 3 minutes, stirring. Add salmon or tuna, cod or haddock, prawns, peas, sweetcorn, capers, chopped herbs and salt and pepper and mix well. Set aside. Put remaining butter, flour and milk in a separate saucepan. Heat gently, whisking, until sauce is thickened and smooth. Simmer gently for 3 minutes, stirring. Cool slightly, then stir in egg yolks and salt and pepper.

Whisk egg whites in a bowl until stiff, then fold them carefully into white sauce. Set aside. Spoon one-third of fish mixture into a shallow ovenproof lasagne dish. Top with three sheets of lasagne. Repeat these layers twice more. Spoon soufflé mixture over lasagne covering it completely. Sprinkle Parmesan over the top. Bake for 35-40 minutes, or until soufflé topping has risen and is golden brown. Garnish with herb sprigs and serve with cooked fresh vegetables.

*Serves 4-6*

# SPINACH CANNELLONI

700g (1½lb) ripe tomatoes, skinned, seeded and
  chopped
2 leeks, washed and sliced
2 sticks celery, finely chopped
200ml (7fl oz) dry white wine
2 tablespoons tomato purée
1 tablespoon mixed ground spices
salt and freshly ground black pepper
500g (1lb 2oz) fresh spinach leaves, washed
12 fresh lasagne sheets
225g (8oz) ricotta cheese
½ teaspoon freshly grated nutmeg
2 eggs, beaten
100g (3½oz) fresh Parmesan cheese, finely grated
2 teaspoons garlic purée
herb sprigs, to garnish

Preheat oven to 180C (350F/Gas 4). Put first
6 ingredients and salt and pepper in a
saucepan and mix well. Bring to the boil,
reduce heat, cover and simmer for 20-25
minutes, stirring occasionally, until vegetables
are tender. Meanwhile, put spinach in a
saucepan with just the water that clings to its
leaves. Cover and cook for 3-4 minutes, or
until just wilted. Drain well, press out excess
liquid and chop roughly. Set aside. Cook
lasagne in batches in a saucepan of lightly
salted water for 2 minutes. Drain, refresh in
cold water, then drain again. Set aside.

Put spinach in a bowl with ricotta, nutmeg,
eggs, 50g (2oz) Parmesan, garlic purée and salt
and pepper and mix well. Lay lasagne out on
work surface and spoon some spinach mixture
along long edge of each sheet. Roll lasagne to
make cannelloni. Arrange cannelloni, seam-
side down, in a shallow ovenproof dish. Purée
tomato mixture in a blender or food processor.
Pour evenly over cannelloni and bake for 30-
40 minutes. Sprinkle with remaining
Parmesan and garnish with herb sprigs.

*Serves 4-6*

# — MEDITERRANEAN LASAGNE —

1 onion, sliced
1 clove garlic, crushed
1 red pepper, seeded and sliced
1 yellow pepper, seeded and sliced
450g (1lb) courgettes, sliced
350g (12oz) mushrooms, sliced
400g (14oz) can chopped tomatoes
2 teaspoons dried herbes de provence
salt and freshly ground black pepper
40g (1½oz) butter
40g (1½oz) plain flour
550ml (20fl oz) milk
1 teaspoon Dijon mustard
115g (4oz) pecorino or Cheddar cheese, grated
9 no pre-cook egg lasagne sheets
25g (1oz) fresh Parmesan cheese, finely grated

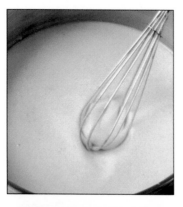

Preheat the oven to 190C (375F/Gas 5). Put onion, garlic, peppers, courgettes, mushrooms, tomatoes, dried herbs and salt and pepper in a large saucepan and mix well. Cover and cook for 10 minutes, stirring occasionally. Meanwhile, melt butter in a saucepan, add flour and cook gently for 1 minute, stirring. Gradually whisk in milk and mustard, then cook, whisking continuously, until sauce is thickened and smooth. Simmer gently for 2 minutes, stirring. Remove the pan from the heat and stir in pecorino cheese, then set aside.

Spoon one-third of the vegetable mixture into an ovenproof lasagne dish and top with 3 sheets of lasagne. Repeat these layers twice more, ending with a layer of lasagne. Pour cheese sauce over the top, covering pasta completely. Sprinkle Parmesan over the top. Bake for 35-40 minutes, or until golden brown and bubbling. Serve with hot crusty garlic bread and a mixed salad.

*Serves 4*

# RATATOUILLE BEAN BAKE

1 red onion, thinly sliced
2 cloves garlic, crushed
1 small aubergine (about 200g/7oz), diced
2 courgettes, sliced
1 yellow pepper, seeded and sliced
175g (6oz) chestnut mushrooms, sliced
400g (14oz) can chopped tomatoes
2 tablespoons tomato purée
4 tablespoons olive oil
2 teaspoons dried herbes de Provence
salt and freshly ground black pepper
400g (14oz) can red kidney beans, rinsed and drained
400g (14oz) can flageolet beans, rinsed and drained
300g (10oz) dried orecchiette
finely grated fresh Parmesan or mature Cheddar
 cheese, to serve

Preheat the oven to 180C (350F/Gas 4). Put onion, garlic, aubergine, courgettes, yellow pepper, mushrooms, tomatoes, tomato purée, olive oil, dried herbs and salt and pepper in a large ovenproof dish and stir to mix well. Cover and bake for 30 minutes. Stir in beans, cover and bake for a further 30-45 minutes, stirring once, until vegetables are cooked and tender.

Meanwhile, cook pasta in a large saucepan of lightly salted boiling water for 12-15 minutes, or until just cooked or al dente. Drain thoroughly. Add pasta to ratatouille and toss well to mix. Serve on warmed plates and sprinkle generously with Parmesan or Cheddar cheese. Serve with fresh crusty bread.

*Serves 4-6*

# — THREE CHEESE MACARONI —

225g (8oz) dried short-cut macaroni
salt and freshly ground black pepper
50g (2oz) butter
50g (2oz) plain flour
700ml (25fl oz) milk
2 teaspoons Dijon mustard
175g (6oz) Cheddar or pecorino cheese, grated
115g (4oz) mozzarella cheese, finely diced
115g (4oz) fresh Parmesan cheese, finely grated
4 tablespoons fresh wholemeal breadcrumbs
marjoram sprig, to garnish

Cook pasta in a large saucepan of lightly salted boiling water for 8-10 minutes, or until just cooked or al dente.

Meanwhile, melt butter in a separate saucepan, add flour and cook gently for 1 minute, stirring. Gradually whisk in milk and mustard and cook, whisking continuously, until sauce is thickened and smooth. Simmer gently for 2 minutes, stirring. Stir in Cheddar or pecorino cheese, mozzarella, 50g (2oz) Parmesan and salt and pepper. Drain pasta thoroughly and add to cheese sauce. Mix well, then transfer to a flameproof dish.

Preheat the grill to high. Mix remaining Parmesan with breadcrumbs and sprinkle over macaroni cheese. Grill for a few minutes or until golden brown and bubbling. Garnish with marjoram sprig, and serve with cooked fresh vegetables such as green beans and baby sweetcorn.

*Serves 4*

VARIATION: Top macaroni cheese with sliced tomatoes, sprinkle breadcrumbs and Parmesan over the top and grill as above.

# - BROCCOLI & COURGETTE BAKE -

225g (8oz) dried penne rigate
salt and freshly ground black pepper
225g (8oz) small broccoli florets
225g (8oz) courgettes, sliced
50g (2oz) butter
50g (2oz) plain flour
700ml (25fl oz) milk
150ml (5fl oz) double cream
200g (7oz) mature Cheddar cheese, grated
2 teaspoons wholegrain mustard
3 tablespoons chopped fresh parsley
2 tablespoons fresh breadcrumbs
15g (½oz) sunflower seeds (optional)
parsley sprigs, to garnish

Preheat the oven to 200C (400F/Gas 6).
Lightly grease an ovenproof dish and set
aside. Cook pasta in a large saucepan of
lightly salted boiling water for 10 minutes,
or until just cooked or al dente. Meanwhile,
cook broccoli and courgettes in a saucepan
of boiling water for 3 minutes. Drain well
and keep warm. Put butter, flour, milk and
cream in a saucepan and heat gently,
whisking continuously, until sauce is
thickened and smooth. Simmer gently for
3 minutes, stirring.

Remove pan from heat and stir in 175g
(6oz) cheese, the mustard, chopped parsley
and salt and pepper. Drain pasta thoroughly
and add to sauce with vegetables. Stir gently
to mix. Transfer to prepared dish. Mix
together remaining cheese, breadcrumbs
and sunflower seeds, if using, and sprinkle
over pasta. Bake for 20 minutes, or until
golden brown and bubbling. Garnish with
parsley sprigs and serve with crusty French
bread and a mixed dark leaf salad.

*Serves 4*

# ── ITALIAN PASTA STIR-FRY ──

350g (12oz) dried spaghetti or bucatini
salt and freshly ground black pepper
2 tablespoons olive oil
1 onion, thinly sliced
2 cloves garlic, crushed
1 red pepper, seeded and sliced
1 yellow pepper, seeded and sliced
3 courgettes, diagonally sliced
4 plum tomatoes, seeded and chopped
150ml (5fl oz) passata
2 tablespoons chopped fresh mixed herbs
85g (3oz) fresh Parmesan cheese, finely grated
herb sprigs, to garnish

Cook pasta in a large saucepan of lightly salted boiling water for 10-12 minutes, or until just cooked or al dente. Meanwhile, heat oil in a wok or large frying pan, add onion and garlic and stir-fry over a fairly high heat for 1 minute. Add peppers and courgettes and stir-fry for 3-4 minutes. Add tomatoes, passata, chopped herbs and salt and pepper and stir-fry for a further 1-2 minutes. Remove the pan from the heat.

Drain pasta thoroughly, add to the wok and toss well to mix. Sprinkle Parmesan cheese over pasta and toss gently to mix. Serve on warmed plates. Garnish with herb sprigs and serve with warm focaccia bread.

*Serves 4-6*

VARIATIONS: Use 2 leeks, washed and sliced, or 6 shallots in place of onion. Use standard tomatoes in place of plum tomatoes.

# —— STUFFED ROAST PEPPERS ——

2 red peppers
2 yellow peppers
3 tablespoons olive oil
1 leek, washed and finely chopped
1 clove garlic, crushed
115g (4oz) mushrooms, finely chopped
175g (6oz) cooked small pasta shapes such as
    tubettini or fusillini
115g (4oz) Cheddar cheese, grated
3 plum tomatoes, chopped
3 tablespoons chopped fresh basil
salt and freshly ground black pepper
basil sprigs, to garnish

Preheat the oven to 180C (350F/Gas 4).
Cut peppers in half lengthways, remove
cores and seeds and place pepper halves on a
baking sheet, hollow-side up. Set aside.
Heat 1 tablespoon oil in a saucepan, add
leek, garlic and mushrooms and cook gently
for 5 minutes, stirring occasionally. Remove
the pan from the heat and stir in cooked
pasta, cheese, tomatoes, chopped basil and
salt and pepper and mix well.

Spoon mixture into pepper halves and
drizzle with remaining oil. Bake for 35-40
minutes, or until filling is golden and
bubbling. Garnish with basil sprigs and
serve with crusty French bread and a mixed
baby leaf salad.

*Serves 4*

VARIATIONS: Use Red Leicester cheese in
place of Cheddar. Use courgettes in place of
mushrooms.

# CHEESE GNOCCHI

2 x 400g (14oz) cans cherry tomatoes
1 red onion, finely chopped
2 cloves garlic, crushed
3 tablespoons tomato purée
1 teaspoon fennel seeds, crushed
1 teaspoon dried chilli flakes, crushed
salt and freshly ground black pepper
700g (1½lb) peeled potatoes, diced
85g (3oz) fresh Parmesan cheese, finely grated
50g (2oz) pecorino cheese, finely grated
25g (1oz) butter
1 egg, beaten
200g (7oz) plain flour
herb sprigs, to garnish

Put tomatoes, onion, garlic, tomato purée, fennel seeds, chilli flakes and salt and pepper in a saucepan. Bring to the boil, then reduce heat and simmer, uncovered, for 25-30 minutes, stirring occasionally, until sauce is thick and pulpy. Meanwhile, make the gnocchi. Cook potatoes in a saucepan of boiling water for 10-15 minutes, or until tender. Drain well, then return to the pan and mash until smooth. Add the Parmesan and pecorino cheeses, butter, egg and salt and pepper and beat until smooth and well mixed.

Add half the flour and mix well, then gradually add remaining flour, until dough is smooth and slightly sticky. Divide in half and roll each piece into a long thin sausage shape, then cut into 2.5-3cm (1-1¼in) lengths. Chill for 30 minutes. Cook gnocchi in batches in a large pan of lightly salted boiling water for 4-5 minutes. Remove from pan using a slotted spoon, and drain well. Serve on warmed plates with tomato sauce spooned over. Garnish with herb sprigs.

*Serves 4-6*

# TOMATO & BRIE BAKE

450g (1lb) cherry tomatoes, halved
3 tablespoons olive oil
4 shallots, thinly sliced
2 cloves garlic, crushed
225g (8oz) button mushrooms, sliced
500g (1lb 2oz) fresh radiatore
salt and freshly ground black pepper
250g (9oz) mascarpone
4 tablespoons chopped fresh basil
225g (8oz) Brie, rind removed and cheese diced
  (weight without rind)
40g (1½oz) fresh Parmesan cheese, finely grated
basil sprigs, to garnish

Preheat oven to 180C (350F/Gas 4). Put tomatoes, cut-side up in a single layer in a large shallow ovenproof dish and drizzle 2 tablespoons oil over. Bake for 10 minutes. Meanwhile, heat remaining oil in a saucepan, add shallots, garlic and mushrooms and cook for 5 minutes, stirring occasionally. Cook pasta in a large saucepan of lightly salted boiling water for 4 minutes, or until just cooked or al dente. Drain thoroughly and return to the rinsed-out saucepan.

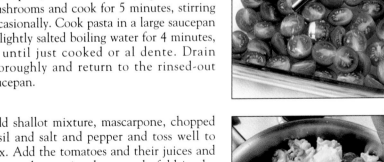

Add shallot mixture, mascarpone, chopped basil and salt and pepper and toss well to mix. Add the tomatoes and their juices and stir gently to mix, then gently fold in the Brie. Transfer mixture to an ovenproof dish. Sprinkle Parmesan over the top. Bake for about 20 minutes, or until the top is golden. Garnish with basil sprigs and serve with a mixed green salad.

*Serves 6*

## COUNTRY-STYLE PASTA

2 tablespoons olive oil
85g (3oz) sun-dried tomatoes in oil
  (drained weight), roughly chopped
175g (6oz) bottled roasted mixed peppers
  (drained weight), cut into thin strips
2 cloves garlic, crushed
300ml (10fl oz) passata
500g (1lb 2oz) fresh riccioli
salt and freshly ground black pepper
4 tablespoons chopped fresh basil
50g (2oz) fresh Parmesan cheese, finely grated
basil sprigs, to garnish

Heat oil in a saucepan, add sun-dried tomatoes, peppers and garlic and cook for 3 minutes, stirring occasionally. Add passata and bring to the boil, then simmer gently, uncovered, for 5 minutes, stirring occasionally. Meanwhile, cook pasta in a large saucepan of lightly salted boiling water for 3 minutes, or until just cooked or al dente. Drain the pasta thoroughly and return to the rinsed-out saucepan.

Stir chopped basil and salt and pepper into tomato sauce, then add to pasta and toss well to mix. Serve on warmed plates and sprinkle with Parmesan. Garnish with basil sprigs and serve with hot crusty garlic bread.

*Serves 4*

VARIATIONS: Use oil from the jar of sun-dried tomatoes in place of olive oil. Use 2-3 tablespoons chopped fresh coriander in place of basil.

# — COURGETTE FRITTATA —

115g (4oz) dried short-cut macaroni
salt and freshly ground black pepper
50g (2oz) butter
1 onion, chopped
1 clove garlic, crushed
2 courgettes, thinly sliced
1 small red pepper, seeded and thinly sliced
115g (4oz) mushrooms, sliced
6 eggs
2 teaspoons dried Italian herb seasoning
115g (4oz) fresh Parmesan cheese, finely grated
herb sprigs, to garnish

Cook pasta in a large saucepan of lightly salted boiling water for 10 minutes, or until just cooked or al dente.

Meanwhile, melt butter in a large non-stick frying pan, add onion, garlic, courgettes, red pepper and mushrooms and cook for 8-10 minutes, stirring occasionally, until softened. Drain pasta thoroughly, then add to vegetables and stir to mix. In a bowl, beat eggs with dried herbs and salt and pepper, then stir in 85g (3oz) Parmesan. Pour egg mixture over vegetables and pasta and stir briefly to mix, spreading the mixture out evenly in the pan.

Cook over a medium heat, without stirring, until eggs are beginning to set and frittata is golden brown underneath. Preheat grill to medium. Sprinkle remaining cheese over the top of the frittata, then grill until top is lightly browned. Cut into wedges to serve and garnish with herb sprigs. Serve with warm ciabatta bread and a mixed dark leaf salad.

*Serves 4-6*

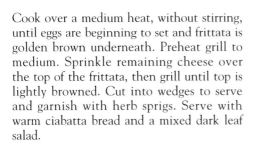

# BAKED MUSHROOM TORTELLONI

70g (2½oz) butter
1 small red onion, finely chopped
1 clove garlic, crushed
225g (8oz) button mushrooms, halved
115g (4oz) mixed fresh wild mushrooms, sliced
40g (1½oz) plain flour
450ml (16fl oz) milk
150ml (5fl oz) single cream
115g (4oz) Dolcelatte cheese, diced
450g (1lb) fresh spinach and ricotta tortelloni
salt and freshly ground black pepper
3 tablespoons chopped fresh flat-leaf parsley
3 tablespoons fresh breadcrumbs

Preheat the oven to 200C (400F/Gas 6). Melt 25g (1oz) butter in a saucepan, add onion, garlic and mushrooms and sauté for 5 minutes. Remove vegetables from the pan using a slotted spoon and place in a sieve over a bowl. Set aside to drain. Add remaining butter to pan and heat until melted. Add flour and cook for 1 minute, stirring. Gradually whisk in milk and cream, then cook, whisking continuously, until sauce is thickened and smooth. Simmer gently for 2 minutes, stirring, then add Dolcelatte cheese and stir until melted.

Meanwhile, cook pasta in a large saucepan of lightly salted boiling water for about 4 minutes, or until just cooked or al dente. Drain thoroughly and return to rinsed-out pan. Add mushroom mixture to pasta with 2 tablespoons chopped parsley, cheese sauce and salt and pepper; toss well to mix. Transfer to an ovenproof dish. Mix remaining parsley and breadcrumbs together and sprinkle over pasta. Bake for 20-25 minutes, or until golden brown and bubbling.

*Serves 4*

# PEPPER & LEEK GRATIN

4 peppers (2 red and 2 yellow)
350g (12oz) dried wholewheat fusilli
salt and freshly ground black pepper
50g (2oz) butter
4 leeks, washed and sliced
1 fresh red chilli, seeded and finely chopped
6 tablespoons crème fraîche
115g (4oz) Emmental cheese, grated
2 tablespoons fresh breadcrumbs
1 teaspoon paprika
herb sprigs, to garnish

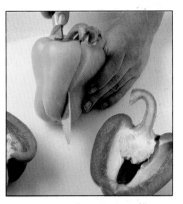

Preheat grill to high. Halve peppers lengthways and put them, cut-side down, on rack in a grill pan.

Grill for 10-15 minutes, or until skins are blackened and charred. Remove from the heat, cover peppers with a clean damp tea towel and set aside to cool. Once cool, remove and discard skin, cores and seeds from peppers and cut flesh into strips. Set aside. Cook pasta in a large saucepan of lightly salted boiling water for 10 minutes, or until just cooked or al dente. Meanwhile, melt butter in a pan, add leeks and chilli and cook gently for 8-10 minutes, stirring occasionally, until softened. Add pepper strips and cook briefly.

Drain pasta thoroughly and return to the rinsed-out pan. Add vegetables, crème fraîche and salt and pepper, and toss well to mix. Transfer mixture to a shallow flameproof dish. Mix together cheese, breadcrumbs and paprika and sprinkle over the top. Grill for a few minutes, or until golden brown on top and bubbling. Garnish with herb sprigs and serve with crusty French bread.

*Serves 4-6*

# —— PANCETTA BEAN SALAD ——

350g (12oz) frozen baby broad beans
350g (12oz) fresh penne rigate
salt and freshly ground black pepper
1 tablespoon olive oil
300g (10oz) pancetta, finely diced
1 clove garlic, crushed
1 bunch spring onions, chopped diagonally
1 yellow pepper, seeded and diced
200ml (7fl oz) passata
2 tablespoons chopped fresh basil
basil sprigs, to garnish

Cook beans and pasta in a pan of lightly salted boiling water for 5 minutes, or until beans are tender and pasta is just cooked or al dente.

Drain thoroughly, set aside and keep warm. Meanwhile, heat oil in a wok or large frying pan, add pancetta and stir-fry for 3-4 minutes. Add garlic, spring onions and yellow pepper and stir-fry for 2-3 minutes, until just tender. Add passata and salt and pepper and stir-fry until hot and bubbling.

Add cooked broad beans, pasta and chopped basil and stir-fry to mix. Serve on warmed plates and garnish with basil sprigs. Serve with warm crusty garlic and herb bread or ciabatta bread.

*Serves 4*

VARIATIONS: Use diced smoked streaky or back bacon or diced chorizo in place of pancetta. Use chopped fresh coriander or flat-leaf parsley in place of basil.

# – CHORIZO & CHICK PEA SALAD –

225g (8oz) dried fusilli
salt and freshly ground black pepper
400g (14oz) can chick peas, rinsed and drained
225g (8oz) cooked chorizo, thinly sliced
225g (8oz) baby plum tomatoes, halved
1 orange or yellow pepper, seeded and diced
115g (4oz) sugar-snap peas, chopped
50g (2oz) rocket leaves
1 bunch spring onions, chopped
6 tablespoons tomato juice or passata
2 tablespoons olive oil
2 teaspoons balsamic vinegar
1 tablespoon chopped fresh mixed herbs
½ teaspoon light soft brown sugar

Cook pasta in a large saucepan of lightly salted boiling water for 10-12 minutes, or until just cooked or al dente. Drain, rinse under cold running water, then drain again thoroughly. Set aside to cool completely. Put cold pasta in a large bowl with chick peas, chorizo, tomatoes, orange or yellow pepper, sugar-snap peas, rocket leaves and spring onions, and toss well to mix.

Put the tomato juice or passata, oil, vinegar, chopped herbs, sugar and salt and pepper in a small bowl and whisk together until thoroughly mixed. Pour over pasta salad and toss gently to mix. Serve with crusty bread rolls.

*Serves 4-6*

VARIATIONS: Use canned red kidney beans or cannellini beans in place of chick peas. Use cucumber or radishes in place of sugar-snap peas.

# — CHICKEN & AVOCADO SALAD —

350g (12oz) fresh radiatore
salt and freshly ground black pepper
115g (4oz) mixed salad leaves
50g (2oz) watercress
25g (1oz) mustard and cress
225g (8oz) skinless, boneless cooked chicken, diced
1 ripe avocado
1 tablespoon lemon juice
8 tablespoons mayonnaise
2 tablespoons chopped fresh parsley
1 teaspoon finely grated lemon zest
parsley sprigs, to garnish

Cook pasta in a large saucepan of lightly salted boiling water for 4 minutes, or until just cooked or al dente.

Drain, rinse under cold running water, then drain again thoroughly. Set aside to cool completely. Put salad leaves, watercress and mustard and cress in a bowl and toss to mix. Divide salad evenly between four plates and set aside. Put cold pasta in a bowl with chicken and stir to mix. Peel, stone and dice avocado, toss it with lemon juice, then add to pasta mixture. Toss to mix.

Put mayonnaise, parsley, lemon zest and salt and pepper in a small bowl and mix well. Spoon dressing over pasta mixture and toss gently to mix. Spoon some chicken and pasta mixture into the centre of each plate of salad. Garnish with parsley sprigs and serve with crusty French bread.

*Serves 4*

VARIATIONS: Use rocket leaves in place of watercress. Use cooked turkey in place of chicken.

# – WARM DUCK FARFALLE SALAD –

225g (8oz) dried farfalle
salt and freshly ground black pepper
85g (3oz) mixed salad leaves
8 spring onions, chopped
1 ripe mango, peeled, stoned and diced or
    thinly sliced
4 tablespoons olive oil
1 tablespoon white wine vinegar
1 teaspoon runny honey
2 tablespoons chopped fresh coriander
1 tablespoon sesame oil
225g (8oz) skinless, boneless duck breast,
    cut into thin strips
115g (4oz) mange-tout, trimmed
1-2 tablespoons toasted sesame seeds, to garnish
    (optional)

Cook pasta in a large saucepan of lightly salted boiling water for 10-12 minutes, or until just cooked or al dente. Meanwhile, put salad leaves, spring onions and mango in a large bowl and toss to mix. Set aside. Put olive oil, vinegar, honey, chopped coriander and salt and pepper in a small bowl and whisk together until thoroughly mixed. Set aside.

Heat sesame oil in a wok or large frying pan, add duck and stir-fry over a high heat for 3-4 minutes. Add mange-tout and stir-fry for a further 1-2 minutes, or until duck is cooked and tender. Drain pasta thoroughly and add to salad leaves with hot duck mixture. Toss gently to mix. Give dressing a quick whisk, then pour it over salad and toss to mix. Spoon on to plates and garnish with a sprinkling of sesame seeds, if liked. Serve with soft bread rolls.

*Serves 4*

# — SMOKED MACKEREL SALAD —

350g (12oz) fresh strozzapretti
225g (8oz) frozen peas
salt and freshly ground black pepper
200g (7oz) can sweetcorn kernels, drained
1 red pepper, seeded and finely diced
1 bunch spring onions, chopped
225g (8oz) skinless smoked mackerel fillets, flaked
6 tablespoons mayonnaise
4 tablespoons plain yogurt
1 tablespoon creamed horseradish
3 tablespoons chopped fresh chives

Cook pasta and peas in a large saucepan of lightly salted boiling water for 4 minutes, or until pasta is just cooked or al dente.

Drain, rinse under cold running water, then drain again thoroughly. Set aside to cool completely. Put cold pasta, peas, sweetcorn, red pepper and spring onions in a large bowl and toss to mix. Add smoked mackerel and toss gently to mix.

Put mayonnaise, yogurt, horseradish, chives and salt and pepper in a small bowl and mix together thoroughly. Spoon over pasta salad and toss to mix. Serve with fresh crusty bread.

*Serves 4*

VARIATIONS: Use smoked trout fillets in place of mackerel. Use chopped fresh parsley in place of chives. Use 1 mild white onion, finely chopped, in place of spring onions.

# SPICY SEAFOOD SALAD

225g (8oz) dried spirali
salt and freshly ground black pepper
175g (6oz) mushrooms, thinly sliced
50g (2oz) watercress, roughly chopped
250g (9oz) cherry tomatoes, halved
2 tablespoons olive oil
2 cloves garlic, crushed
1 tablespoon Cajun seasoning
400g (14oz) packet frozen mixed seafood, defrosted
6 tablespoons passata
2 tablespoons dry sherry
1 tablespoon light soy sauce
1 tablespoon tomato purée
herb sprigs, to garnish

Cook pasta in a large saucepan of lightly salted boiling water for 10-12 minutes, or until just cooked or al dente. Meanwhile, put mushrooms, watercress and cherry tomatoes in a salad bowl and stir to mix. Set aside. Heat oil in a wok or large frying pan, add garlic and Cajun seasoning and stir-fry over a fairly high heat for 30 seconds. Add seafood and stir-fry for about 5 minutes, or until cooked.

Mix together the passata, sherry, soy sauce, tomato purée and salt and pepper. Add to the wok and stir-fry until hot and bubbling. Drain pasta thoroughly, add to the wok and stir-fry to mix. Add to the salad bowl and toss well to mix. Garnish with herb sprigs and serve with hot crusty garlic bread.

*Serves 4*

VARIATIONS: Use fresh oyster mushrooms in place of standard mushrooms. Use rocket leaves in place of watercress.

# LAYERED PASTA SALAD

225g (8oz) dried farfalle tricolore
salt and freshly ground black pepper
6 tablespoons olive oil
3 tablespoons pesto
400g (14oz) can salmon, drained, boned and flaked
½ cucumber, sliced
1 large beef tomato, sliced
1 bunch spring onions, finely chopped
1 yellow pepper, seeded and finely diced
115g (4oz) sugar-snap peas, chopped
herb sprigs, to garnish

Cook pasta in a large saucepan of lightly salted boiling water for 10-12 minutes, or until just cooked or al dente.

Drain, rinse under cold running water, drain again thoroughly and set aside to cool completely. Put oil, pesto and salt and pepper in a bowl and whisk together until thoroughly mixed. Add cold pasta and toss well to mix. Add salmon and stir gently to mix. Put one-third of salmon pasta in a glass serving bowl. Arrange cucumber and tomato slices over pasta.

Top with half of remaining salmon pasta to cover cucumber and tomato slices completely. Mix spring onions, yellow pepper and sugar-snap peas together and scatter over pasta. Top with the remaining salmon pasta, covering vegetables completely. Cover and chill for about 1 hour before serving. Garnish with herb sprigs and serve with mini soft bread rolls.

*Serves 6*

# — FOUR-BEAN PASTA MEDLEY —

225g (8oz) dried tricolore or wholewheat fusilli
salt and freshly ground black pepper
115g (4oz) French beans, halved
175g (6oz) frozen baby broad beans
400g (14oz) can borlotti beans, rinsed and drained
200g (7oz) can red kidney beans, rinsed and
  drained
1 red pepper, seeded and diced
1 small mild white onion, thinly sliced
115g (4oz) button mushrooms, sliced
125ml (4½fl oz) passata or tomato juice
2 tablespoons olive oil
1 tablespoon balsamic vinegar
1 clove garlic, crushed
2 tablespoons chopped fresh coriander
baby spinach leaves or chicory leaves, to serve

Cook pasta in a large saucepan of lightly salted boiling water for 10-12 minutes, or until just cooked or al dente. Meanwhile, cook French beans in a separate saucepan of boiling water for 2 minutes, add broad beans, return to the boil and boil for a further 3-4 minutes, or until beans are cooked and tender. Drain pasta and beans, rinse under cold running water and drain again thoroughly. Set aside to cool completely.

Put cold pasta and cooked beans in a large salad bowl, add canned beans, red pepper, onion and mushrooms and toss well to mix. Put passata or tomato juice, oil, vinegar, garlic, chopped coriander and salt and pepper in a small bowl and whisk together until thoroughly mixed. Pour over pasta salad and toss well to mix. Serve on a bed of spinach or chicory leaves. Serve with warm ciabatta bread.

*Serves 4-6*

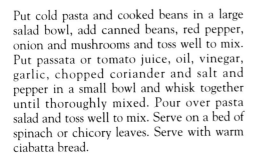

# INDEX